Practical Lean Leadership

A Strategic Leadership Guide for Executives

Bob Emiliani

The Center for Lean Business Management, LLC
Wethersfield, Connecticut

The Center for Lean Business Management, LLC
Wethersfield, CT
Tel: 860.558.7367   www.theclbm.com

Cover design and page layout by Tom Bittel, bittlwrks@aim.com
www.dadsnoisybasement.com

Library of Congress Control Number: 2007903932

Emiliani, M.L., 1958–

Practical Lean Leadership: A Strategic Leadership Guide for Executives / M.L. Emiliani

Includes bibliographical references and index
1. Business   2. Leadership   3. Lean management

I. Title
ISBN-13: 978-0-9722591-5-6

First Edition   January 2008

Ordering information
www.theclbm.com

Made in the U.S.A. using print-on-demand technology.

Lean Behaviors®, Behavioral Waste®, and The Center for Lean Business Management® are registered trademarks of The CLBM, LLC

For Michael and AilUJ

and

The Five

Contents

Preface

Many senior managers are discovering that Lean is much more than a "manufacturing thing." They are learning that Lean is a comprehensive system of management for any type of enterprise, whether it is a for-profit, non-profit, government, or non-governmental organization. They are also recognizing that the Lean management system [1] applies to every part of a business, is often a core element of corporate strategy, and that the executive team has a vital role to play in its success.

Despite the tremendous amount of time, money, and effort that has been applied by managers and associates to achieve a Lean transformation, there are only a few companies that have had notable success with Lean management. That's after over 30 years of effort by tens of thousands of managers in thousands of companies. It would be generous to characterize this as a lackluster showing. The question is: Why have so many efforts fallen flat and what can be done to improve?

According to a survey of management trends [2], only 22 percent of executives are extremely satisfied with their company's Lean efforts. That leaves 78 percent who are dissatisfied. The dissatisfaction is often driven by misunderstandings and misperceptions that remain stubbornly attached to Lean management and prevent its successful application.

While we are finally moving away from comprehending Lean as a "manufacturing thing" or as "tools for the manager's tool kit" to achieve short-term cost reduction, 99 percent of executives are still uninformed when it comes to understanding the leadership challenges associated with practicing Lean management.

They think that by dint of their past work or leadership experiences they are prepared to lead a Lean transformation. But that is not at all the case. The leadership skills and capabilities that they presently have are almost certainly not the ones they will need to lead a Lean transformation. In fact, most are the exact opposite of what they must possess.

The reality is that Lean businesses must be led differently – and with few exceptions, executives have not been properly trained to lead a Lean business. It is not surprising that success with Lean management has been so limited. The purpose of this workbook is to teach executives how to correctly lead a Lean transformation and achieve greater business success. Readers should have some prior knowledge of Lean principles, practices, and tools, but those who do not can still benefit greatly from this workbook.

I was fortunate to notice certain key elements of the leadership challenge when I started learning Lean management in the summer of 1994. At that time I was a business unit manager at Pratt & Whitney in Rocky Hill, Conn., where Shingijutsu consultants were facilitating shop floor kaizen and teaching us Lean principles and practices. Soon thereafter I embarked on 13-year effort to understand the intricacies of Lean leadership and how it differs from the leadership of conventionally-managed businesses.

What I found over the years from my own practice of Lean management in industry and through careful study and observation was truly striking. I wrote up my ideas and findings on Lean leadership in over a dozen papers published in practitioner-oriented management journals. These papers have steadily gained acceptance among Lean leaders. Four papers have been recognized by the University of Toyota as helpful resources for Toyota associates learning The Toyota Way, including

"Lean Behaviors," "Linking Leaders' Beliefs to their Behaviors and Competencies," and "Using Value Stream Maps to Improve Leadership."

My work has simplified while at the same time advanced leadership far beyond the common understandings and training methods used for leadership development, yet remains fully consistent with Lean principles and practices. However, the papers I wrote are burdened by certain editorial requirements that make them less accessible to readers. The intent of this workbook is to overcome these limitations and create a helpful resource for Lean management practitioners.

I would like readers to know that my years of industry and management experience have had a great and lasting influence on my efforts to help people understand Lean leadership. The problems that I dealt with were the same or similar to the ones you are dealing with. I have always focused on practical aspects and producing work that is useful in the real world and have purposefully chosen to leave theory to others.

Lean management has two key principles: "Continuous Improvement" and "Respect for People." Unfortunately, most executives only sponsor continuous improvement efforts and are unaware of or disregard the "Respect for People" principle. This workbook focuses on both principles and particularly on the interplay between them from a leadership perspective. It provides the essential information that executives need to know if they desire to correctly understand Lean management and lead a Lean transformation.

Chapters 1-10 present an easy-to-follow, step-by-step Lean leadership development process for executives, starting with understanding fundamental concepts to daily practice to performance feedback. Along the way, you will learn that Lean leadership involves much more than just changing some behaviors.

Readers are asked to answer questions and complete various exercises at the end of each chapter to strengthen their understanding of Lean leadership and management, often in comparison to their conventional leadership and management practices. In addition, information is highlighted which must be committed to memory for it to be useful in the daily practice of Lean management.

Executives who wish to become credible Lean leaders should have realistic expectations regarding what this workbook will do for them. It will not turn executives into genuine Lean leaders just by reading it. This workbook is a step on the challenging, fun, and rewarding journey to becoming a Lean leader, which requires both intellectual and physical leadership. It is a very important first step because it provides you with the proper foundation for advancement. You will need to practice what you learn in this workbook every day, without fail. A key challenge will be for you to balance Lean thinking with Lean doing.

Finally, readers may notice that the tone of this workbook is no-nonsense and at times very direct [3]. Please be assured that the intent is not to disparage, but instead to awaken, stimulate, and open minds to entirely new ways of understanding and practicing leadership.

Bob Emiliani
December 2007
Wethersfield, Conn.

Acknowledgments

I would like to sincerely thank the team who volunteered to share their time to review the manuscript and provided dozens of valuable suggestions for improvement: Arthur Byrne, Orest Fiume, Thomas Goetter, James Huntzinger, Brian Maskell, Edward Miller, Jon Miller, Kevin Meyer, and Helen Zak. Substantial changes were made as a result of their comments, which certainly yielded a better and more useful book.

I also thank executives who have attended my Lean leadership training courses and my former graduate students – almost all of whom were full-time working professionals with management responsibilities – for the helpful feedback they have given me over the last 10 years.

Emerald publishing has been very supportive of my work, most of which breaks from conventional views of leadership. This puts special demands the journal editors who must wade through conflicting feedback from reviewers and make tough final decisions. I would like to thank John Peters and Marie McHugh, the editors of *Management Decision* and *Leadership and Organizational Development Journal*, respectively. Over the years they have recognized my work as innovative and practical contributions to the field of leadership.

I would also like to thank Doi Yoshihisa, my first sensei, who taught me kaizen heart and mind; LET who served as an excellent role model for Lean leadership; and LET, EES, and Pratt & Whitney for giving me the opportunity to learn and apply Lean principles and practices in the shop, office, and supply chains, and as a leader.

I wish to acknowledge fine work of the multi-talented Tom Bittel, the behind the scenes team member who does the hard work of turning my manuscripts into books, and to Mary Milewski for copyediting the manuscript.

Finally, special thanks to ME and JE for all the fun and good times; to Lucinda for 22 years of listening to my ideas, giving me new insights, and supporting my work; and to CE, who I think of every day.

Introduction

Awareness of Lean among senior managers began to blossom in the late 1980s and gained significant momentum in the mid-1990s. Many good sources of information in the form of experienced consultants and books written by academics and Lean management practitioners [1] became available to senior managers. But somewhere along the way, the word Lean began to take on new meanings and has been practiced in ways that resulted in bad outcomes for many companies, or its employees, suppliers, investors, and the communities in which the business operates.

Lean is now viewed negatively by many people, which adds a layer of complexity to its introduction or spread within an organization. How did this happen? In simple terms, managers led Lean efforts using the same leadership beliefs, behaviors, and competencies that they used before they embarked on their Lean journey. A critical part of this is the inadvertent extension of a conventional zero-sum view of business into the practice of Lean management.

The term "zero-sum" is an important one and will be used frequently in this workbook [2]. It means:

> **When one party gains at the expense of others.**

Simple examples of zero-sum interactions include when a powerful buyer squeezes a supplier's profit margin in order to obtain short-term unit price savings, or when employees are laid off after having made improvements in how they perform their work. This is not how Lean businesses manage costs or their employee or supplier relationships.

Left uncorrected, the misunderstandings and misapplications of Lean will lead to its demise. Lean management will not go away entirely, but its practice will be limited to a few companies whose leaders prefer to follow the beat of a different drummer – the customer – and various Lean tools will become subsumed into general management practice.

It is a major challenge to accurately represent Lean management to current and future management practitioners and to help ensure that they do not make errors that will cause their Lean efforts to fall short of expectations or fail completely. A large part of this challenge is to present the leadership dimension of Lean management.

When confronted with the challenge to learn about Lean leadership, most executives turn to well-worn conventional approaches to leadership development that tend to be more rooted in the view that leadership is principally an art. The problem with conventional approaches is that they usually lack specificity, are disconnected from the actual workplace, or are difficult to make actionable. They typically include:

- Listening to other executives' war stories
- Self-assessments
- Competency models
- Simulations
- Role Playing
- Mentoring

While these may be helpful in small ways, they are not what executives need in order to become Lean leaders.

This workbook will present proven approaches to understanding leadership and leadership development in ways that are practical yet powerful, and can be more easily grasped and put into practice compared to traditional approaches – and always in the context, language, and methods of Lean management. It is critically important to maintain very close ties to Lean because it enables executives to comprehend ideas and practice methods that are closely connected to what is happening in the actual workplace every day.

Lean management has its origins in scientific thinking and the scientific method [3]. Creating approaches to Lean leadership development that are closely aligned with the Lean mindset and Lean principles and practices results in new view of leadership as more science than art. Importantly, this makes the abstract nature of leadership tangible, which has never been done until now. This means that Lean leadership is now accessible to many more managers than is the case when leadership is viewed narrowly as an art.

Over the years I have made a conscious effort to ensure that the new approaches to leadership development that I created [4-8] – which are firmly rooted in my own real-world management experience, not theory – are very specific and easy to make actionable. Otherwise, what good would they be? However, it is ultimately the top executives who must accept the challenge to learn and practice these new things, evolve, and grow. If they do not accept the challenge, then it makes no difference if the approach to leadership development is closely tied to Lean or not, or if it is specific and actionable or not.

The concepts and tools that executives can use daily to practice and demonstrate Lean leadership are presented in Chapters 4, 5, and 7.

> • **Lean Behaviors**®
> • **Continuous Personal Improvement**™
> • **Leadership Beliefs-Behaviors-Competencies**
> • **Standardized Work for Executive Leadership**

Please note that expanding certain Lean tools into the domain of leadership development is not intended to lend support to the perception that Lean management is nothing more than tools. Instead, they are used as innovative and practical devices to help executives better understand the principles and key objectives of the Lean management system. They also serve as aids in comprehending the required leadership beliefs, behaviors, and competencies, and to clearly inform executives of what they must do differently every day.

The motivation by executives to adopt Lean is many and varied. Some want to improve overall corporate competitiveness and customer satisfaction [9] while others are just tired of the waste, re-work, and aggravation. Many adopt Lean to increase profits, or for more selfish reasons such as to grow their personal wealth. However, managers, consultants, and academics rarely give thought to the personal benefits that managers can realize if they practice Lean correctly. I would like to point these out because they lead to significant improvements in the quality of life at work. You will experience:

- Better focus
- Clear purpose and consistent direction
- Less emphasis on "making the month"
- Fewer mistakes
- Run the business using simple principles and simpler metrics that focus on what really matters
- Fewer meetings, reviews, and reports
- Better decisions based on better data and simpler analyses
- Distributed problem recognition, analysis, and improvement
- More effective decentralized decision making
- Fewer surprises and less firefighting
- More trust
- Calmer atmosphere
- Fewer anxieties
- More fun

There are many benefits, including health benefits, for yourself and others – if you do Lean management right. Executives cannot simply bolt Lean knowledge onto their existing base of business knowledge and leadership capabilities to gain access these benefits. They will have to question some of their basic beliefs about business and leadership and be willing to modify or let go of a substantial amount of their current business knowledge. This may sound crazy or intimidating, but executives who understand and practice Lean management correctly find it liberating and invigorating.

The key will be to understand the difference between REAL Lean and Fake Lean, as shown in the figure below [10]. The image on the left shows a partial, defective representation that is commonly in use today, while the image on the right shows the principles that form the complete Lean management system.

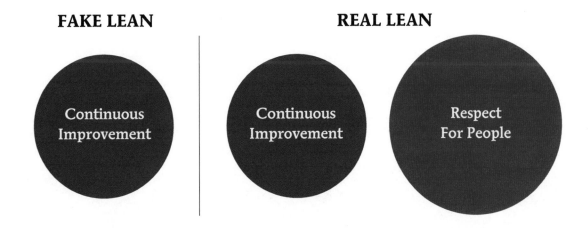

In summary, the advantages of the approaches to leadership development contained in this workbook include:

> - **Understand leadership as more science than art**
> - **Consistent with Lean principles and practices**
> - **Connected to the actual workplace**
> - **Practical**
> - **Easy to understand**
> - **Specific and actionable**
> - **Customer-first perspective**

Finally, this workbook can be used individually or used by the leadership team in a self-paced group training activity. Either format will significantly advance your knowledge of strategic leadership and how to lead a Lean transformation.

Introduction – Self-Study

Write your responses in the space provided. Answer these questions to the best of your ability, recognizing that in some cases you may not have all the necessary information.

 Thinking

1. What was your impression of Lean when you first became aware of it?

2. Have you had bad experiences with Lean? If so, what caused the bad experiences?

3. What does "Continuous Improvement" mean to you? How do you define it?

4. What does "Respect for People" mean to you? How do you define it?

5. Why do you think Toyota represents the "Respect for People" principle as a larger circle compared to the "Continuous Improvement" principle?

6. Has your company been practicing Fake Lean or REAL Lean? If the answer is Fake Lean, then what do you think caused the incorrect practice of Lean management?

7. Identify five reasons why you think the "Respect for People" principle is so important in the practice of Lean management.

-
-
-
-
-

8. If someone says to you "Lean is a theory," what would you say to them to convincingly refute that perception?

9. Describe ways in which laying people off as a result of productivity improvements would be inconsistent with the "Respect for People" principle.

Doing

1. Identify three concrete steps you will take to improve your practice of the "Respect for People" principle, where people are employees, suppliers, customers, investors, and the communities in which your business operates.

Action Plan*

Who	Will Do What	By When

* Make sure you do not delegate that which only you should do.

Commit These to Memory

- Lean management is a principle-based management system. The two principles are: "Continuous Improvement" and Respect for People."

- Lean is a non-zero-sum system of management where all parties share in the gains (or losses).

- There are right ways and wrong ways to understand and implement the Lean management system.

1

What is
Lean Management?

Chapter Highlights

- Understand Lean as a management system
- Lean principles and key objectives
- Definitions of waste, unevenness, and unreasonableness

Leaders wanting to lead a Lean transformation must first possess an accurate understanding of what Lean management is and what it is not.

"Lean" was the name that researchers gave to Toyota's system of manufacturing management in the mid-1980s [1]. Toyota refers to it as the "Toyota production system," which is a sub-set of their over-all management system called "The Toyota Way" [2, 3]. Companies that seek to emulate Toyota's management system are said to be practicing Lean management.

Lean management is defined as [4]:

> **A non-zero-sum principle-based management system focused on creating value for end-use customers and eliminating waste, unevenness, and unreasonableness using the scientific method.**

But what is a system? It is:

> **An organized and consistent set of principles and practices.**

Companies that practice the Lean management system can do so in ways that are either high or low fidelity representations of Toyota's management system. In most cases Lean management, as it has been understood and practiced thus far by companies other than Toyota, is an ultra-low or low fidelity version of Toyota's management system. Not surprisingly, the results they achieve are very poor compared to Toyota.

Lean is a management system comprising two key principles:

> **Continuous Improvement**
> **and**
> **Respect for People**

It embodies key objectives such as:

> **Creating Value for End-Use Customers**
> **Stable Long-Term Growth**
> **Balance**
> **Harmony**
> **Innovation**

And it uses various tool and processes that support the principles and key objectives.

Figure 1-1 shows how Lean management must be understood as a prerequisite for its correct practice. In most companies the focus has been on the application of Lean processes and tools, with little or no regard to the principles or key objectives. Often the tools or processes have been "cherry picked" from the larger system, which leads to very poor results. Companies that cherry pick the tools are practicing Fake Lean, not REAL Lean. Figure 1-1 shows only a partial list of Lean processes and tools. For many years people have thought of Lean in various narrow senses such as "Lean is a manu-

Figure 1-1

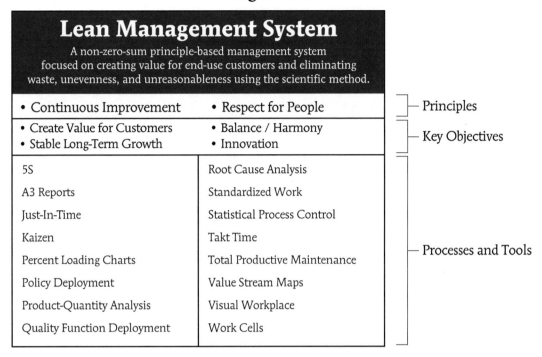

facturing thing." People who are not in manufacturing businesses or who do not work in a manufacturing department use this as an excuse to avoid having to think about or practice Lean management.

A better way to comprehend Lean management is to think of it in its broadest sense:

> **Customer requirements are satisfied by a network of connected services whose basic unit is information.**

Thus, Lean can work wherever information is exchanged. The correct practice of Lean views the existence of internal customer-supplier relationships as well as external customer-supplier relationships, in a non-zero-sum context. In other words, the next process is the customer.

Lean is a management system that is designed to be responsive to buyers' markets, which is what all businesses face unless they have a monopoly. Many top executives adopt Lean management with a sellers' market attitude, or with policies, metrics, and practices in place that inadvertently promote an internal company view that a sellers' market exists. This is a fundamental error in the understanding and practice of Lean management that is inconsistent with the "Respect for People" principle and will undercut "Continuous Improvement" efforts, which will lead to poor results.

Lean management possesses many concepts that are not found in conventional management. This includes the concept of *waste*. Waste is defined as [5]:

> **Any activity that consumes resources but creates no value for the customer.**

Who is the customer? It is the end-use customer; the customer that pays for and uses the product or service that an organization produces. The value proposition for intermediate customers, such as distributors, should also be considered. Intermediate customers, as well as internal customers, serve important roles as partners who collaborate with each other to satisfy end-use customers.

Figure 1-2 shows a very important image that lies at the heart of Lean management [6]. It is the recognition that there is work that adds value for end-use customers, work that is necessary at the present time but does not add value (also called Type 1 waste), and waste that can be eliminated (also called Type 2 waste).

Figure 1-2

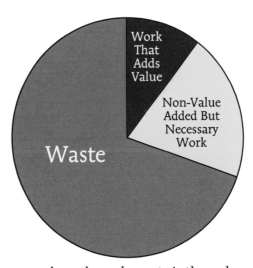

The way to recognize and separate these three elements is through process improvement activities such as kaizen. A primary focus of kaizen is the elimination of waste and to achieve flow. The literal translation of kaizen is:

> **"Change for the better"**
> *in a multilateral context.*

Understanding kaizen more narrowly as "continuous improvement" can invite confusion and lead to the misapplication of kaizen in a unilateral, or zero-sum context. Doing so would violate the "Respect for People" principle. Thus, the change must be non-zero-sum; it must good for all stakeholders. In contrast, a change that is good for the company or its shareholders but bad for employees, suppliers, or customers is not kaizen. A change that is good for engineering but bad for manufacturing or sales is not kaizen.

Kaizen does not exist in conventional management practice, so it is not surprising that the three elements shown in Figure 1-2 are not recognized or understood. In conventional management practice, just about any activity done by anyone is considered value-added. There is no conception of non-value-added but necessary work (under current conditions), and waste is only understood in a very casual way, such as: "That's a waste of time" or "Don't waste your effort."

Kaizen applied to processes that have been designed under conventional management thinking and practices shows that 80 to 90 percent of the work is waste, and only 5 to 10 percent of the work is value-added. The executives who run conventionally-managed businesses do not recognize this, which explains why the company is slow to respond to changes in the buyers' marketplace and perpetually suffer from high cost, low quality, long lead-times, and customer dissatisfaction.

Figure 1-3 lists the seven wastes identified by Taiichi Ohno and his associates at Toyota Motor Corporation [7], which have long been part of Lean management. The boundaries between manufacturing and service are shown simply for clarity and should not lead you to rigidly think of Lean management in terms of categories such as manufacturing or service.

Figure 1-3

WASTE	MANUFACTURING	SERVICE
1. Defects	Scrap / Reworked Parts	Errors in Documents
2. Transportation	Parts Movement	Transport of Documents
3. Overproduction	Making More Than Can Be Sold	Doing Work Not Needed
4. Waiting	People Waiting	Reviews and Approvals
5. Processing	Processing Itself	Processing Itself
6. Movement	Searching for Tools	Searching for Information
7. Inventory	Work-In-Process and Finished Goods	Backlog of Work

In addition to waste, there are two more very important concepts in Lean management that also do not exist in conventional management: *unevenness* and *unreasonableness*. Unevenness is defined as:

> **Work activities or information that fluctuate significantly.**

Unreasonableness is defined as:

> **Overburdening people or equipment.**

All employees, including top leaders, use Lean tools and processes every day to eliminate waste, unevenness, and unreasonableness. However, thinking of Lean management just as "tools for the manager's toolkit" means that an organization will obtain only one-third to one-half the benefit of Lean management. There is no way an organization can become a skilled Lean management practitioner with half or more of the benefit left behind.

A particular challenge for executives is to eliminate waste, unevenness, and unreasonableness in their own work activities and to be highly responsive to workers when they need senior managers to remove or change policies and practices to help eliminate waste, unevenness, and unreasonableness.

Eliminating waste, unevenness, and unreasonableness greatly improves an organization's responsiveness to changes in the buyers' marketplace. It also makes work much more enjoyable.

Chapter 1 – Self-Study

Write your responses in the space provided. Answer these questions to the best of your ability, recognizing that in some cases you may not have all the necessary information.

 Thinking

1. What misunderstandings does your company leadership (CEO or president) have about Lean?

2. What misunderstandings do you have about Lean?

3. What misunderstandings do supervisors and workers in your company have about Lean?

4. Identify five ways your company operates that is consistent with Lean management.

-
-
-
-
-

5. Identify five ways your company operates that is inconsistent with Lean management.

-
-
-
-
-

6. Why are the key objectives of stable long-term growth, balance, and harmony so important to Lean leaders in their practice of Lean management?

7. Identify 12 examples of *waste* in your company or department.

-
-
-
-
-
-

-
-
-
-
-
-

8. Identify 10 examples of *unevenness* in your company or department.

-
-
-
-
-

-
-
-
-
-

9. Identify 10 examples of *unreasonableness* in your company or department.

-
-
-
-
-

-
-
-
-
-

10. It is likely that the senior management team professes to be customer-focused, reflecting views that your company serves a buyers' market. Can you identify company or department-level policies, practices, or metrics that instead channel managers and workers into thinking or behaving as if your company serves a sellers' market?

11. Why is it correct to say "kaizen," and incorrect to say "kaizen event" or "kaizen blitz?" What meaning will be conveyed to people if kaizen is referred to as an "event" or "blitz?"

12. Identify 10 misunderstandings that people in your company have about Lean management. Determine the root cause for the top two misunderstanding using the 5 Whys method (see Appendix I), and identify practical countermeasures that will eliminate the misunderstanding. (Note: In Lean management, countermeasures are not thought of as solutions because it is virtually impossible for people to completely understand a problem at any given point in time. Instead, countermeasures are practical actions based upon current knowledge of the problem that should prevent recurrence).

-
-
-
-
-

-
-
-
-
-

Misunderstanding #1:

Question	Answer	Countermeasure*
1. Why...		•
2.		•
3.		•
4.		•
5.		•
6.		•
7.		•
8.		•
9.		•
10.		•

* Identify a total of 2-3 practical countermeasures.

Misunderstanding #2:

Question	Answer	Countermeasure*
1. Why...		•
2.		•
3.		•
4.		•
5.		•
6.		•
7.		•
8.		•
9.		•
10.		•

* Identify a total of 2-3 practical countermeasures.

13. Identify 10 barriers that have made it difficult for your company to correctly practice Lean management. Determine the root cause for the top two barriers using the 5 Whys method, and identify practical countermeasures that will eliminate the barriers.

- •
- •
- •
- •
- •

- •
- •
- •
- •
- •

Barrier #1:

Question	Answer	Countermeasure*
1. Why...		•
2.		•
3.		•
4.		•
5.		•
6.		•
7.		•
8.		•
9.		•
10.		•

* Identify a total of 2-3 practical countermeasures.

Barrier #2:

Question	Answer	Countermeasure*
1. Why...		•
2.		•
3.		•
4.		•
5.		•
6.		•
7.		•
8.		•
9.		•
10.		•

Identify a total of 2-3 practical countermeasures.

Doing

1. Develop an implementation schedule for the countermeasures you identified in thinking exercises 12 and 13.

Action Plan*

Who	Does What	By When

Make sure you do not delegate that which only you should do.

Commit These to Memory

- Lean management is a non-zero-sum principle-based management system focused on creating value for end-use customers and eliminating waste, unevenness, and unreasonableness using the scientific method.
- Customer requirements are satisfied by a network of connected services whose basic unit is information.
- Waste is any activity that consumes resources but creates no value for the customer.
- Unevenness is work activities or information that fluctuate significantly.
- Unreasonableness is overburdening people or equipment.
- Kaizen means "change for the better," in a multilateral context.
- Do not add the word "event" or "blitz" to kaizen.

2

How Lean Leaders Think

Chapter Highlights
• How conventional leaders think
• How Lean leaders think
• Guidelines for executive decision making

Most Lean implementation problems are caused by a failure to understand the true intent and meaning of Lean management. Executives are at a great disadvantage from the very start of their Lean efforts if they do not possess the correct "basic way of thinking." There are many facets to this [1-3], and several are presented below. However, it is the responsibility of Lean executives to deepen their understanding of the "basic way of thinking" through never-ending study and practice of Lean management.

Executives steeped in conventional management practice tend to lead from the office, rather than from where the work is actually performed. If they came up through the ranks, then there is a tendency to think: "Been there, done that" or "I've paid my dues." As a result, they lose touch with the workers and the work, and get annoyed when workers make mistakes. They also tend to make decisions based on data which can easily be manipulated to look better, compared to making fact-based decisions using a combination of data and actually observing what is happening in the workplace in a non-blaming way. Thus, the basic way of thinking for most managers with respect to leading and decision making is flawed. The basic way of thinking for Lean leaders is:

> **Lean leaders observe the work, "go see" when problems arise and make fact-based decisions.**

Many executives who want to adopt Lean establish a definite time frame for becoming Lean. It is common for them to want to achieve world class status in two or three years. This is consistent with the short-term view that most executives possess, regardless of the era they lived in. However, short-term thinking is inconsistent with executives' other view that the company should remain in business decades into the future. Thus, the basic way of thinking for most managers with respect to time horizon is flawed. The basic way of thinking for Lean leaders is:

> **Lean leaders think long-term.**
> **They do not sacrifice the long-term to secure short-term gains.**

While short-term gains are regularly achieved in Lean management, short-term thinking is not the driver for senior management's decision making.

Executives also fail to recognize that adopting Lean management means that they will be doing something dramatically different from what they have done in the past. Let's look at an example. Say you are currently good at a sport such as bowling or playing a musical instrument such as the tuba – metaphors for the current way of doing business. But now you decide to embark on a journey to learn something new, say golf or guitar – metaphors for the new way of doing business. What is the likelihood that you will become world class in two years? It is impossible, even if you worked 16 hours a day at your new avocation.

You must be realistic and recognize that you might attain advanced beginner's status, or maybe even become an intermediate-level player if you practiced every day, without fail, which most people will not do. It is idealistic to think that you could reach the end-point of being world-class. Performing at that level takes many more years of practice, and there is no permanence to world class status. Failure to practice every day will result in backslide. Thus, the basic way of thinking for most managers with respect to how long it takes to become skilled at practicing Lean management is flawed. The basic way of thinking for Lean leaders is:

> **Lean leaders focus on continuous improvement, not on achieving an end-point.**

The fact that it takes years to understand Lean management does not deter Lean leaders. They realize they will be at work for many years to come, and they want customers to be satisfied and the business to prosper long after they are gone. So they just march forward, one step at a time, with their heads up and eyes wide open so they can observe what is happening in the workplace.

Having attained the highest levels in an organization, executives tend to think there is not much more for them to learn; that the foundational knowledge and capabilities they possess are more-or-less invariant. Lean management proves otherwise; that much of the knowledge we possess actually leads to average or less-than-average outcomes. There is a large disconnect between the rhetoric of excellence that executives espouse versus the knowledge, capabilities, and processes that are in daily use. Executives should not underestimate the extent to which they are learning something completely new. Thus, the basic way of thinking for most managers with respect to learning is flawed. The basic way of thinking for Lean leaders is:

> **Lean leaders enjoy challenging their views and are willing to learn new things.**

The ability to challenge one's views and learn new things is often undercut by large egos and desires for special privileges. There is nothing wrong with having a healthy ego. But it becomes a problem when it interferes with listening and learning. Thus, the basic way of thinking for most managers with respect to sense of self-worth is flawed. The basic way of thinking for Lean leaders is:

> **Lean leaders are humble people who have little interest in special privileges.**

People in general tend to be selfish, and executives are no exception. They often act as if they were taught an iron-clad rule by a former boss or in business school that they should not share the wealth with any stakeholder other than investors. No such rule exists; it is a matter of choice. Executives who transfer wealth from one stakeholder to another are practicing conventional zero-sum management. Lean leaders recognize that better long-term results are achieved through collaboration and sharing. Rather than dividing up slices of a fixed size pie, the pie steadily gets bigger for everyone, including investors. Thus, the basic way of thinking for most managers with respect to sharing in business is flawed. The basic way of thinking for Lean leaders is:

> **Lean is a non-zero-sum system of management, and must be practiced that way faithfully.**

People are often left out in the drive to secure good economic results. The perception that executives have about people, workers and suppliers in particular, is often laden with negative biases and stereotypes. Lean is a management system that seeks to balance human and economic interests. After all, it was people who created business, not lions or sharks, to satisfy their interests. Success in business requires attitudes and actions that demonstrate respect towards employees, suppliers, customers, investors, and the communities in which they operate. Thus, the basic way of thinking for most managers with respect to the role of people in business is flawed. The basic way of thinking for Lean leaders is:

> **People must be respected.**

While respecting people sounds simple enough, is in fact very challenging to executives under pressure. Hence, most leaders do an extremely poor job of respecting people. Executives will need to take up the challenge to understand how their policies, practices, metrics, beliefs, and behaviors disrespect people, and make appropriate changes to be consistent with Lean principles and practices. For example, metrics and policies are often inwardly focused and inconsistent with what customers really want. Lean leaders scrutinize business metrics to make sure they measure what customers care about and do not have policies that lead to customer complaints. Thus, the basic way of thinking for most managers with respect to customers is flawed. The basic way of thinking for Lean leaders is:

> **Customer first.**

Most executives implicitly or explicitly favor local or point optimization of the individual parts of the business because it appears as if progress is being made. They also hope that the sum of the improvements made in each department results in a better business overall. That is a leap of faith, a necessary one, but only because conventional management education and practice does not teach future executives how to improve the entire business.

By improving individual parts in isolation, they are forced to make undesirable trade-offs, the evidence of which is in the metrics that each department uses to optimize its own performance. Nobody can honestly claim that the purchase price variance metric can exist in harmony with the defects-per-million quality metric. Destructive trade-offs are always made between these two metrics in conventional management practice. This is just one of many examples. Executives must carefully scrutinize their business metrics to ensure they do not create waste.

Lean is not a system for making trade-offs as is conventional management. The kaizen process teaches people how to achieve better results; the simultaneous reduction of cost and lead-time, and improvement in quality and worker safety, performance, and satisfaction. Thus, the basic way of thinking for most managers with respect to improvement as being a set of necessary trade-offs is flawed. The basic way of thinking for Lean leaders is:

> **Lean management is not a system of trade-offs.**
> **It is how the entire business is improved.**

That begs the question, what is improvement? In conventionally-managed businesses, executives will often cite major purchases such as a new software system or new machines as evidence of improvement. But did these purchases eliminate waste, unevenness, or unreasonableness? Did they increase costs or reduce costs? Did they restrict flexibility or improve flexibility? Did it make it harder for people to do the work, or easier? Did it put the system in control of people, or are the people in control of the system? It should be obvious; people must control the system, but they will have difficulty doing this if they don't understand their reason for existence.

Noticeably absent in conventional management is an explicit statement of corporate purpose: the reason for a company's existence. Lean executives view not having a corporate purpose as a failure on their part to give meaning to people's work. They see corporate purpose as an essential component of good corporate governance. Without it, management decision making will be inconsistent and create waste [4, 5]. Thus, the basic way of thinking for most managers with respect to corporate purpose is flawed. The basic way of thinking for Lean leaders is:

> **Corporate purpose must be clearly defined.**

A zero-sum corporate purpose, such as "our purpose is to maximize shareholder value" or "our purpose is to make money" is inappropriate for Lean management and will lead to waste, unevenness, and unreasonableness, and entrenched conflicts between key stakeholders.

Executives of conventionally-managed businesses often trivialize the importance of business by referring to it as a "game" or in war-like terms, which is a telling indicator of how deep the roots of zero-sum thinking run. It also diminishes the reality that business is a human centered activity whose purpose, broadly speaking, is to balance and satisfy both human and economic interests. Lean leaders do not refer to business as a "game" or in war-like terms because it carries connotations that do not accurately portray their view of business nor the meaning or intent of Lean management. Thus, the basic way of thinking for most managers with respect to how they represent business to employees and other stakeholders is flawed. The basic way of thinking for Lean leaders is:

> **Business is a serious activity that is of great importance to people and should not be trivialized by its leaders.**

Finally, a common mistake make by executives is to view the "soft skills" of conventional leadership behaviors as separate from the "hard skills" of conventional management practice, as shown in Figure 2-1 (left side). When hard times arrive, they decide to transition to Lean, principally by adopting selected Lean tools, and carry forward the same view that "soft skills" of conventional leadership behaviors are separate from the "hard skills" of Lean management practice (middle). This will only lead to failure. The correct view is that Lean leadership behaviors are very closely connected to Lean principles and practices and that they work together (right side). Thus, the basic way of thinking for most managers with respect to the relationship between "soft skills" and "hard skills" is flawed. The basic way of thinking for Lean leaders is:

> **Lean soft skills and Lean hard skills are connected and they work together.**

Figure 2-1

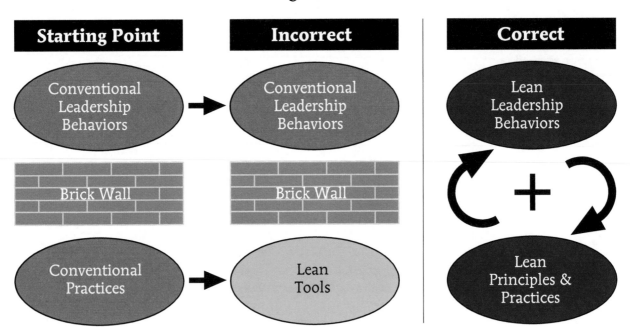

In summary, the "basic way of thinking" of Lean leaders is very different from that possessed by executives of conventionally-managed businesses. Once again, it is the responsibility of Lean executives to deepen their understanding of the "basic way of thinking" through never-ending study and practice of Lean management.

Executives who wish to create a Lean enterprise must challenge their basic way of thinking. There is no shortcut, and it will be hard for most leaders to do this because it runs counter to what they have been previously taught and how they have previously managed and led their organizations. You have to be tired of the status quo and motivated to want to do better. The upside is that it will be very enjoyable and rewarding to learn and practice the Lean management system [3, 6-8].

Chapter 2 – Self-Study
Write your responses in the space provided.

 Thinking

1. Do you "go see" when a problem arises? If you do, is your presence interpreted by others as blaming or judgmental? How would that be problematic?

2. Identify five data-driven decisions you have made that turned out to be wrong because you missed important facts.

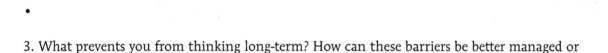

-
-
-
-
-

3. What prevents you from thinking long-term? How can these barriers be better managed or removed entirely?

4. Do you prefer to achieve "quick hits" and "home runs," or steady improvement in small increments? Why?

5. When was the last time you challenged your thinking on a deeply held business policy or practice. What was the subject matter?

6. Are you fond of the special privileges of executive life? In what ways could they be a liability to your leadership?

7. Do you view business as a zero-sum activity? Who did you learn this from? How do you know it is true?

8. What principles does the President or CEO use to manage the business? Do you use these same principles? Are they zero-sum or non-zero-sum?

9. What kinds of trade-offs do you routinely make in your company or department? Would your business be better without having to make such trade-offs? Would your customers, employees, and suppliers be happier?

10. Do you have a corporate purpose? Is your corporate purpose explicit or do you have to figure it out based on management's patterns of decision making?

11. Is your company's corporate purpose zero-sum or non-zero-sum? Is it consistent with Lean principles?

12. In what ways is your "basic way of thinking" different from a Lean executive's "basic way of thinking?"

13. In what ways will a Lean executive's "basic way of thinking" yield better business and personal outcomes?

Doing

1. In order to change my basic way of thinking, I will:

Action Plan*

Do What	By When *

Make sure you do not delegate that which only you should do.

2. Develop a one-sentence non-zero-sum corporate purpose that is consistent with Lean principles.

Commit These to Memory

Lean leaders:
- Observe, "go see" when problems arise, and make fact-based decisions.
- Think long-term.
- Are committed to never-ending continuous improvement.
- Like to challenge conventional views and learn new things.
- Are not arrogant.
- Practice Lean as a non-zero-sum management system.
- Believe business stakeholders must be respected.
- Have a "customer first" attitude.
- Are skeptical of the need for trade-offs.
- Define corporate purpose.
- Do not trivialize business.
- View "soft" and "hard" skills as connected.

3

A Better Definition of Leadership

Chapter Highlights

- Traditional definitions of leadership
- Shortcomings of traditional definitions
- A new definition of leadership for Lean leaders

One of the things Lean management seeks to do is reduce or eliminate variation because variation is waste and leads to the creation of more waste. The practice of leadership itself suffers from a tremendous amount of variation. Followers are quick to notice the variation in leadership exhibited by their senior managers. They know the difference between those leaders who take their responsibilities seriously and those who simply don't care but act like they do. This variation leads to inconsistent direction, half-hearted efforts, and slow execution. Yet managers are always telling their people that time is precious, problems must be fixed quickly, and opportunities must be acted upon.

The definition of leadership also suffers from a tremendous amount of variation. There are several dozen definitions in existence which emphasize different aspects of leadership and convey a wide range of meanings. This reflects the many different ways in which leadership has been conceptualized since the leadership of business organizations became a formal topic of study in the early 1900s. It is common to find that each member of a leadership team possesses a different definition of leadership, which introduces significant variability within an organization and leads to uneven executive and corporate performance.

The definition of leadership that is used is very important because it serves as a guide for people in leadership positions to help them better understand their role. The best-known definitions of leadership can be widely interpreted by people in leadership positions. For example, John Maxwell's definition of leadership is [1]:

"Leadership is influence – nothing more, nothing less."

Peter Drucker's definition of leadership is [2]:

"The only definition of a leader is someone who has followers."

Warren Bennis' widely quoted definition of leadership is [3]:

"Leadership is a function of knowing yourself, having a vision that is well
communicated, building trust among colleagues, and taking effective action
to realize your own leadership potential."

But there are many problems with these common definitions, including:

- They lack sufficient detail to know precisely what to do
- They focus on the leader and not the followers, the customers of leadership
- Leaders can interpret them in many different ways

But most importantly, both good and bad leaders can satisfy these definitions, which render them useless. For example, the corrupt former leaders of Enron, Rite-Aid, Sunbeam, or Parmalat had influence, they had no difficulty building trust among colleagues, they were able to communicate a vision, and the actions they took helped them realize their leadership potential.

In this workbook we will use an improved definition of leadership; one that is practical, more specific and actionable, and better captures the essence of Lean leadership. It is less concerned with leaders' personal attributes and more focused on the effects that leaders should have on others in the performance of their daily activities.

The improved definition of leadership is [4]:

> **Beliefs, behaviors, and competencies that demonstrate respect for people, motivate people, improve business conditions, minimize or eliminate organizational politics, ensure effective utilization of resources, and eliminate confusion and rework.**

This definition includes critical aspects of leadership that are not contained in other definitions, as well as specific items that are usually not practiced by executives daily. It suggests to leaders that they eliminate waste and inefficiency and avoid marginalizing the interests of key stakeholders in order to develop trust. It also begins to inform leaders that a principal part of their function is to facilitate information flows, not to slow down or block them.

The view that a principal role of leadership is to facilitate information flows between people is unique and plays a very important role in being an effective Lean leader. This will be discussed in greater detail in Chapters 4-7, as well as how to make each of the items contained in improved definition of leadership come alive.

Carefully study Maxwell's, Drucker's, and Bennis' definitions of leadership. It is those definitions that most executives have in mind when they lead. However, are those definitions leading to favorable impressions of business and its leaders? In general, the answer is "No." The public at large has negative views of business and business leaders, while employees at lower levels often feel disrespected, unmotivated or de-motivated; business conditions are deteriorating or are increasingly uncertain; that organizational politics is rampant; resources are not utilized effectively; and people are confused and engaged in seemingly endless re-work.

The improved definition of leadership challenges executives to take the next step forward in the evolution of their understanding and practice of leadership – a step that will be challenging but also within reach. It maintains a practical focus relative to desirable human and economic characteristics in business. In other words, the improved definition is serious and business-like, and not frivolous or idealistic.

The improved definition should help change your understanding of the leaders' role in a Lean business. Maxwell's, Drucker's, and Bennis' definitions of leadership are simply insufficient for executives who wish to lead Lean businesses.

Chapter 3 – Self-Study
Write your responses in the space provided.

 Thinking

1. Identify 10 ways in which Emiliani's improved definition of leadership is preferable to Bennis' definition of leadership for leading a Lean business.

-                               •
-                               •
-                               •
-                               •
-                               •

2. Give eight specific examples of how your leadership creates waste, unevenness, or unreasonableness.

-                               •
-                               •
-                               •
-                               •

3. Give eight specific examples of when your leadership style has slowed down or blocked the flow of information between people.

-                               •
-                               •
-                               •
-                               •

Doing

1. Identify aspects of your leadership that you will improve on to eliminate waste, unevenness, or unreasonableness?

Action Plan*

Leadership Problem	Corrective Action	By When

* *Make sure you do not delegate that which only you should do.*

2. What aspects of your leadership will you improve upon to improve the flow of information among people?

Action Plan*

Leadership Problem	Corrective Action	By When

* *Make sure you do not delegate that which only you should do.*

Commit These to Memory

- Emiliani's Lean leadership definition: Beliefs, behaviors, and competencies that demonstrate respect for people, motivate people, improve business conditions, minimize or eliminate organizational politics, ensure effective utilization of resources, and eliminate confusion and rework.
- One of the leader's principal roles is to get information to flow among people within the company and between the company and its suppliers, customers, investors, and communities.

4

Lean Leadership Behaviors

Chapter Highlights

- How Lean leaders behave
- Value-added behaviors and behavioral waste
- Lean behaviors and continuous personal improvement

Careful observation of the companies where Lean management prospers, compared to where it has struggled or failed, reveals that success is strongly dependent on the types of behaviors exhibited by senior managers. Successful Lean leaders know that they must be consistent; if they tell employees to eliminate *process* waste, then the leaders must not *behave* in wasteful ways. If they behave in wasteful ways, then it sends a contradictory, de-motivating message that workers recognize and then use to avoid investing their hearts and minds into the daily application of Lean principles and practices.

In companies that struggle with Lean management or have failed, one always finds tremendous amounts of wasteful behaviors exhibited by the executive team. Recall Figure 1-2, which shows that only a small portion of the work is value added, some work is non-value-added but necessary (under current conditions), and the remainder is waste. Conventional management practice does not recognize the existence of waste. If executives don't recognize the existence of *process* waste, why would they ever recognize the existence of their own *behavioral* waste? It turns out they don't recognize the existence of their behavioral waste even after they are well into their Lean transformation. This error typically goes uncorrected for years and undercuts the company's Lean efforts, which then leads to the executives' dissatisfaction with Lean management. Instead, executives should be dissatisfied with their understanding and practice of Lean management.

Figure 4-1 shows the behavioral analogue to Figure 1-2. It shows there are leadership behaviors that add value, leadership behaviors that are non-value-added but necessary or unavoidable (under current conditions), because people are not perfect, and wasteful leadership behaviors. Just as in Figure 1-2, a large portion of leadership behaviors are waste, while only a small portion of leadership behaviors are value-added. The value-added behaviors are what workers expect from their leaders; behaviors that motivate them to willingly and enthusiastically become engaged in applying Lean principles and practices.

Figure 4-1

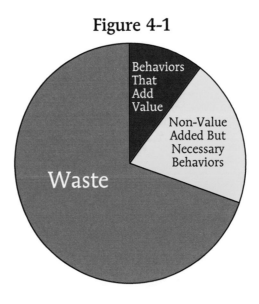

The beauty of Figure 4-1 is its simplicity and total consistency with Lean management. If you can remember Figure 1-2 as it pertains to work activities, then you can easily remember Figure 4-1 as it pertains to leadership behaviors. This will be an important first step in your practice of the behaviors that are *required* to lead a Lean transformation.

Executives who have grown up with conventional management practice often motivate employees through threats or intimidations, sometimes subtle and sometimes in-your-face, any typically use faulty metrics and policies that initiate wasteful behaviors in others. These behaviors lead to organizational dysfunction that makes it almost impossible for a company to respond to its many business and human resource challenges.

The common remedy is to send executives to expensive and elaborate leadership development programs that feature emotional intelligence or leadership competency models. These are intended to cure the ills that are characteristically found in conventionally-managed businesses. In contrast, Lean leaders do not have much use for these expensive leadership training and development programs because they implicitly or explicitly understand that their behaviors cannot be wasteful.

Figure 4-2 shows the original seven wastes, plus one more. The eighth waste is called "behavioral waste" [1]. Some people characterize the eighth waste as the "waste of creativity," "underutilizing worker talents," or "waste of people." However, performing a root cause analysis of why creativity, talents, or people are wasted reveals that the root cause is "behavioral waste" exhibited by the executive team.

Behavioral waste is not some abstraction related to a theory of leadership. Rather, it is a real phenomenon that will cause great harm if efforts are not made to recognize and eliminate it. Its existence in the real world is supported by the fact the Lean management specifically identifies "Respect for People" as one of its two key principles.

Figure 4-2

WASTE	MANUFACTURING	SERVICE
1. Defects	Scrap / Reworked Parts	Errors in Documents
2. Transportation	Parts Movement	Transport of Documents
3. Overproduction	Making More Than Can Be Sold	Doing Work Not Needed
4. Waiting	People Waiting	Reviews and Approvals
5. Processing	Processing Itself	Processing Itself
6. Movement	Searching for Tools	Searching for Information
7. Inventory	Work-In-Process and Finished Goods	Backlog of Work
8. Behaviors	Behaviors that consume resources but create no value for customers	

Why is it important to eliminate behavioral waste among members of the executive team? Because it blocks the flow of information, undermines teamwork, causes delays and re-work, focuses people's attention on problem avoidance and obfuscation, lowers job satisfaction, and makes it much more difficult to satisfy customers. Behavioral waste demonstrates disrespect for people, which is obviously inconsistent with the "Respect for People" principle.

Some examples of value-added behaviors, non-value-added but necessary (or unavoidable) behaviors under current conditions, and behavioral waste are shown in Figure 4-3.

Figure 4-3

Value-Added Behaviors	Non-Value-Added But Necessary (or Unavoidable) Behaviors	Behavioral Waste
Humility	Gossip	Blame
Calmness	Short-Term Thinking	Office Politics
Wisdom	Ignorance	Confusion
Patience	Inconsistency	Inconsistency
Objectivity	Negative Thoughts	Unknown Expectations
Balance	Biases	Revenge
Trust	Stereotypes	Elitism

Items listed in each column are not intended to correspond to items listed in other columns.

The non-value-added but necessary (or unavoidable) behavior category is waste; it is called Type 1 behavioral waste. These leadership behaviors exist because people are not perfect. Notice that "inconsistency" appears in both the non-value-added but necessary (or unavoidable) behaviors and behavioral waste categories. Why is that? It is because leaders may exhibit small inconsistencies that will not be too bothersome to other people. But sometimes the inconsistencies are great and will cause lots of problems that consume resources and add no value.

Type 1 behavioral waste is difficult for most leaders to quickly comprehend and therefore hard for them to figure out what to do about it. You would not want to completely eliminate non-work related conversations, for example, but in some cases they can be disruptive or consume valuable time. Any of the items that appear in the non-value-added but necessary (or unavoidable) behaviors category can easily shift over into the behavioral waste category depending upon circumstances and other people's perceptions.

The behavioral waste category, called Type 2 behavioral waste, gives examples of leadership behaviors that are obviously waste and which must be eliminated. Leaders' main focus initially should be on eliminating Type 2 behavioral waste. As learning progresses, they will begin to comprehend Type 1 behaviors as waste and start to think what, if anything, they need to do to modify or eliminate those behaviors.

Executives should desperately want to exhibit value-added behaviors because they result in numerous important benefits including:

- Improve information flow
- Enable people to learn
- Facilitate engagement in improvement activities
- Improve responsiveness
- Cause fewer errors
- Focus people on understanding and responding to problems

The problem is that most executives think they do not exhibit any wasteful behaviors. Let's check that view against the reality of our past work experiences. It is likely that you have had eight to 12 different bosses since you have been in the workforce. Of the many bosses you have had, how many of them were really good? People typically say one or two were good, while the remaining bosses ranged from mediocre to awful.

Now think of the behavioral characteristics of your best bosses. It is likely that they exhibited value-added behaviors, while your worst bosses exhibited lots of behavioral waste. You did not request these bad behaviors; they were *pushed* onto you. Typically 10 to 20 percent of bosses exhibit mostly value added behaviors, 50 percent exhibit an inconsistent and confusing mix of value-added and wasteful behaviors, and the remainder exhibit toxic levels of behavioral waste [2].

Say you could place an order requesting certain specific types of behaviors from your boss. What would they be? Would you create a list of value-added behaviors, a list of wasteful behaviors, or a mix of the two? Would you include in the list: "I want a boss that blames me and humiliates me in front of others?" Of course not; you would create a list that contained only value-added behaviors. By developing this list and communicating it with your boss you'd be creating *pull* for the desired value-added behaviors.

A central practice in Lean management is to respond to the pull of customers and engage only in the value-added activities to satisfy customer demand. Similarly, the leaders of an organization should respond to the pull of its employees – the customer of leadership services – and engage only in the value-added activities to satisfy customer demand. Indeed, employees have a list of value-added behaviors in their minds but they are usually unwilling to communicate it to management because they fear the consequences of expressing their honest views. This is just one example of how behavioral waste cuts off the flow of information.

In addition, executives usually never ask employees to articulate the value-added behaviors that they expect to see. So the pull for value-added behaviors goes unrecognized by senior managers, and the result is perpetuation of behavioral waste over the long-term, which invariably leads to periodic corporate financial or non-financial distress. Note that periodic corporate financial or non-financial distress is a repetitive error whose root causes will point to the existence of behavioral waste and failure to practice the "Respect for People" principle.

Let's not forget that in addition to leadership behaviors that are waste, there are also *uneven* and *unreasonable* leadership behaviors. Unevenness can be more broadly defined as:

> **Work activities, information, or leadership behaviors that fluctuate significantly.**

The definition of unreasonableness remains unchanged:

> **Overburdening people or equipment.**

So what must aspiring Lean leaders do? They must:

> **Determine and respond to the pull of employees regarding the leadership behaviors they expect to see.**

The same applies to suppliers and other stakeholders. After all, investors would not want a leadership team to be in conflict with key value-adding constituents, its employees and suppliers, nor with its cash-generating customers. Yet this is often the case. Employees are viewed stereotypically as nothing more than labor or as a cost, suppliers are often seen as the enemy, and customers are viewed narrowly as just sources of revenue. The total cost of conflict between the company and these key stakeholders will surely be much higher than the total cost of cooperation.

You may not like to hear that you must determine and respond to the pull of employees regarding your leadership behaviors. You may think that it is in conflict with your job to create shareholder value – which it is not. (Note: your job is not to *maximize* shareholder value because that is a zero-sum objective which will end up destroying shareholder value). Sometimes you have to do things that you may not want to do in order to achieve a worthwhile objective. Take a practical analogy: if you want to become a good guitar player, you must practice every day. Practice is not something that most people like to do, but it is a fundamental requirement if one wishes to achieve the objective of becoming a good guitar player.

A particularly insidious type of behavioral waste is blame, which instills fear in people and causes them to become distracted, lose focus, and be quiet. There are two types of blame: overt and covert. Overt blame is the obvious type of blame that anyone can see, while covert blame is hidden and more difficult to see. Executives who blame people for problems choke off the flow of information, and therefore cannot claim they are using resources effectively. Additionally, executives who would like employees to innovate better and faster must eliminate overt and covert blame. It is easy to eliminate overt blame. Eliminating covert blame is harder to do, but it must be done.

Behavioral waste is so destructive to Lean management that we have to figure out how to eliminate it. So how do we do it? There are different ways that leaders can eliminate behavioral waste. The first method is to understand which of their behave are waste. This can be done using information from traditional performance appraisals, 360 degree feedback, or similar instruments. Executives would simply recognize these behaviors as waste, make a daily commitment to eliminate their use, and then obtain feedback to assess whether or not any improvement has occurred. The problem with this approach, however, is that most executives would find it difficult to do.

A better method is to practice Lean behaviors [1]. This is an adaptation of the five-step thinking process that James Womack and Daniel Jones presented in their 1996 book *Lean Thinking* regarding production activities [3], but instead it is re-cast in human terms as shown in Figure 4-4:

Figure 4-4

Lean Behaviors

1. Specify Value
I seek to understand the expectations of people I interact with regardless of position or status. I consider the perspectives of key stakeholders (associates, suppliers, customers, investors, community).
2. Identify the Value Stream
I understand which of my behaviors add value and which are waste, and how my behaviors impact business processes and value creation for end-use customers. I strive to achieve non-zero-sum gains.
3. Flow
I understand how my leadership behaviors can create errors, delays, confusion, and re-work. I think about how to do my work in less time to help improve work flows. I am not an impediment to information flow.
4. Pull
I understand the pull signals that my key stakeholders give me. I strive to do what is wanted, when it is wanted, in the amount wanted, and where it is wanted.
5. Continuous Improvement
I work to eliminate behavioral waste. I continuously improve my understanding of behavioral waste and strive to eliminate it to facilitate information flow.

The beauty of this approach is that if you understand each of the five items in a production sense, then it is a simple extension to understand and apply it as a method for leadership development.

As discussed in Chapter 1, Lean tools and processes are used to eliminate waste, unevenness, and unreasonableness. We can use the exact same tools and processes to eliminate executives' behavioral waste, unevenness, and unreasonableness. Figure 4-5 illustrates the concept for Lean leadership development, called "continuous personal improvement" [4]:

Figure 4-5

Lean Process Improvement Tool		**Lean Leadership Improvement Tool**
• Continuous Improvement	⟶	• Continuous Improvement
• One Piece Flow	⟶	• One Piece Flow
• Standardized Work	⟶	• Standardized Work
• Kanban	⟶	• Kanban
• Five S's	⟶	• Five S's
• Visual Controls	⟶	• Visual Controls
• Audio Signals	⟶	• Audio Signals
• Total Productive Maintenance	⟶	• Total Productive Maintenance

Figure 4-6a presents Lean tools used in manufacturing or service operations [5], while Figure 4-6b describes the analogue of how each of the Lean tools can be used for Lean leadership development [4].

Figure 4-6a

Continuous Improvement in Operations

One-Piece Flow
Making and moving one piece at a time.
Standardized Work
Establishing precise procedures for work in a production process.
Kanban
A signaling device that authorizes and instructs people for the production or withdrawal of items in a pull system.
The Five S's
Disciplined habits of organization and cleanliness in the workplace.
Visual Controls
Management of a workplace that enables the status and performance to be ascertained at a glance.
Audio Signals
Sounds in the workplace used to indicate abnormal conditions.
Total Productive Maintenance
A set of techniques used to ensure that machines are able to perform work when they are needed.

Figure 4-6b

Continuous Personal Improvement

One-Piece Flow
I understand the value-added part of my work. I am able to perform my work as it comes to me, mostly without delay. I think of how to eliminate waste in my own daily activities.
Standardized Work
I am consistent in my words and actions. I strive to reduce variation in interpretation of my intent. I treat people the same regardless of level.
Kanban
I respond to signals from stakeholders to provide what is needed, when it is needed, in the amount needed, and where it is needed.
The Five S's
My mind, work habits, and workplace are well-organized.
Visual Controls
I seek to eliminate facial expressions and body language that signal disinterest or distrust.
Audio Signals
The tone, volume, pace, inflection, and timing of my voice is used effectively to signal positive interest or support.
Total Productive Maintenance
I try to improve my personal effectiveness by maintaining my mind and body. I achieve good balance between work, family, and personal interests.

Once again, the beauty of this approach is its simplicity and consistency with Lean management. If you understand each of the seven tools and practices in a production sense, then it is a simple extension to understand and apply them as tools for leadership development. You need to remember only one language and one set of concepts and tools – and they are specific, actionable, and practical.

Lean Leadership Behaviors

This is an improvement over other approaches to leadership development, which most executives find very difficult to use in actual business settings because it requires them to understand and integrate the "hard skills" of business and the "soft skills" of emotional intelligence, for example. The task of integrating these two skills is usually the nexus of failure, so executives will naturally want to focus their efforts on the "hard skills" of business. This will inadvertently block the flow of information because other peoples' needs will not be met.

Overall, the approach to leadership development presented in Figures 4-1, 4-4, and 4-6b is unique in that it is completely consistent with the Lean management. Aspiring Lean leaders now have a fully integrated management system – inclusive of principles, concepts, methods, and tools for business process improvement *and* leadership development. Having only one thing to remember and apply will be much easier to do.

The recognition that many leadership behaviors are waste – that they add cost but do not add value and can be eliminated – coupled with Lean behaviors and continuous personal improvement tools, constitutes a truly elegant countermeasure to the problem of leadership behaviors that are grossly inconsistent with Lean management principles and practices.

However, do not fool yourself into thinking that you can understand the meaning of

- Waste, unevenness, and unreasonableness
- Specify value, identify the value stream, flow, pull, and continuous improvement
- One piece flow, standardized work, kanban, 5S, visual control, audio signals and total productive maintenance

in a production *or* leadership sense simply by reading about it. Executives must become engaged as team members in shop or office floor kaizen, after which they will be better understand what each these things mean and how they can be applied to Lean leadership development. It will take time and practice, but the benefits will be great.

Figure 4-7 shows the joining together of Figures 1-2 and 4-1, which yields a unified system for understanding value-added, non-value-added but necessary, and waste in the context of both work activities and leadership behaviors. Once again, it is simple to understand and easy to remember, which will help make it easier for executives to use in daily practice. This is done by constantly asking:

> **Does this leadership behavior add value or is it waste?**

If the behavior is value-added, then how is it so? What objective real-world evidence exists to inform you that this is a value-added behavior? If the behavior is waste, then how is it so, and what countermeasures can you put in place to reduce or eliminate the wasteful behavior? The ability to ask these questions over and over again and act upon the answers requires careful observation of cause-and-effect and attention to detail that can only come through daily practice.

Simple visual controls can be very helpful for reminding executives of the questions that they should be asking themselves every day [6].

Figure 4-7

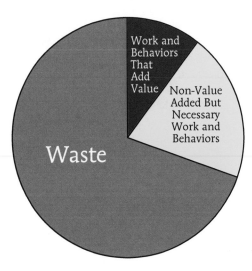

Figure 4-8 shows the mindset that executives steeped in conventional management must work hard to develop. They must accept that improvement in work processes and leadership behaviors occurs in a methodical step-by-step fashion, similar to the manner in which one learns to play golf or the piano. "Home runs" and "quick hits" are not the language of Lean management because they promote a dysfunctional focus on short-term thinking. In addition, few executives consider if the "quick hits" they seek result in "quick losses" elsewhere in the organization or among their key stakeholders.

You certainly take home runs or quick hits that might happen to come your way, but they are not the focus of people's Lean efforts. While your competitors are hoping for home runs and quick hits, you will be methodically moving forward and will eventually go past them. Whether or not you stay past them is the topic of Chapter 5.

Figure 4-8

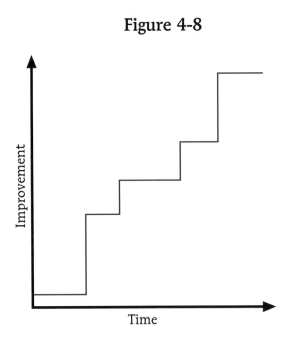

Chapter 4 – Self-Study
Write your responses in the space provided.

 Thinking

In exercises 1-5, be sure you do not get confused between human behaviors and work activities (e.g. meetings).

1. Identify 10 value-added leadership behaviors (in addition to those in Figure 4-3).

-                •
-                •
-                •
-                •
-                •

2. Identify 10 leadership behaviors that are waste (in addition to those in Figure 4-3).

-                •
-                •
-                •
-                •
-                •

3. Identify eight non-value-added but necessary or unavoidable leadership behaviors (in addition to those in Figure 4-3).

-                •
-                •
-                •
-                •

4. Identify 10 examples of uneven leadership behaviors.

-
-
-
-
-

      -
      -
      -
      -
      -

5. Identify 10 examples of unreasonable leadership behaviors.

-
-
-
-
-

      -
      -
      -
      -
      -

6. Identify 10 examples of how behavioral waste cuts off the flow of information.

-
-
-
-
-

      -
      -
      -
      -
      -

7. Identify five examples of overt blame and five examples of covert blame.

Overt	Covert
•	•
•	•
•	•
•	•
•	•

8. Identify your top five personal (not organizational) barriers that prevent implementing Lean behaviors (Figure 4-4) and identify two practical countermeasures for each barrier.

Barrier	Rationale	Countermeasure

9. Identify your top five personal (not organizational) barriers that prevent implementing the continuous personal improvement tools (Figure 4-6b) and identify two practical countermeasures for each barrier.

Barrier	Rationale	Countermeasure

10. Identify seven organizational barriers that prevent implementing Lean behaviors (Figure 4-4) or continuous personal improvement tools (Figure 4-6b). Identify two practical countermeasures for each barrier.

Barrier	Rationale	Countermeasure

11. Explain why it would be inappropriate to mandate Lean behaviors (Figure 4-4).

12. Explain why it would be inappropriate to provoke behavioral waste in other people.

13. Explain why it would be inappropriate to think that developing Lean behaviors (Figure 4-4) can be a "quick hit."

14. Explain why it would be inappropriate to create a new and unique Lean behaviors metric [7].

15. Explain why dialogue, discussion, and debate are necessary to identify and correct problems, and for creativity in business, and how these types of communication can be consistent or inconsistent with Lean behaviors or the "Respect for People" principle.

16. Describe how blaming employees or suppliers benefits your end-use customers. Is blame a value-added feature that your customers ask for? Do your customers want to pay for the delays and re-work caused by blame?

17. Describe how organizational politics benefit your end-use customers. Is organizational politics a value-added feature that your customers ask for? Do your customers want to pay for the delays and re-work caused by organizational politics?

Doing

1. Identify your top three behavioral wastes and identify corrective actions.

Action Plan*

Behavioral Waste	Corrective Action	By When

Make sure you do not delegate that which only you should do.

Commit These to Memory

- Behavioral waste is defined as leadership behaviors that consume resources but create no value for customers and can be eliminated.
- Behavioral waste demonstrates disrespect for people and is inconsistent with the "Respect for People" principle.
- Eliminating behavioral waste improves information flow internally and between the company and its suppliers customer, investors, and communities.
- Executives must respond to the pull for value-added behaviors that employees expect.
- Blaming employees or suppliers and perpetuating a political workplace creates no value for end-use customers.
- Figures 4-1, 4-2, 4-3, 4-4, 4-6b, and 4-8.

5

Value Stream Maps as a Leadership Development Tool

Chapter Highlights

- A new use for value stream maps
- Conventional leadership beliefs, behaviors, and competencies
- Lean leadership beliefs, behaviors, and competencies

The previous chapter should have been very enlightening in how it provided simple constructs for understanding leadership behaviors that are fully consistent with Lean principles and practices. Helpful as it may be, it is does not fully illuminate the scope of the differences between the minds of conventional leaders compared to Lean leaders. For that we must turn to value stream maps, but use them in a way that is very different from how they are normally used.

Value stream maps, originally called "material and information flow diagrams," are one-page depictions of the process used to make a product [1, 2]. They were first developed by the Operations Management Consulting Division of Toyota Motor Corporation, Toyota City, Japan, in the late 1980s. Value stream maps help people identify ways to get material and information to flow without interruption, improve productivity and competitiveness, and implement system wide rather than isolated improvements. For over 10 years, value stream maps were applied to manufacturing activities. They are also now used to understand the flow of material and information in office activities [3] such as human resources, legal, new product development, and financial reporting. Indeed, they can be used to map any service business process.

Value stream maps are created by cross-functional teams of people who are directly involved in the process under consideration. There are two principal types of value stream maps: "current state" and "future state." As the name implies, current state value stream maps depict the current way in which material and information are processed. Until a current state map is drawn, people – especially top executives – are unaware of the large amount of waste that exists in a process as well as the confusing information signals. Future state value stream maps depict a future condition that incorporates yet-to-be-made improvements via kaizen.

The use of value stream maps has been extended to the field of accounting to determine the process costs of a value stream. The information contained in value stream maps can be used to calculate current and future state process costs and create value stream profit-and-loss statements [4]. This is a significant break from traditional cost accounting methods, and one that more accurately reflects the costs associated with production and non-production activities. Value stream maps have also been used to determine the amount of carbon dioxide greenhouse gas generated by processing and transportation [5].

The use of value stream maps has been extended to a fourth practical application; the field of leadership development. It is a new route for identifying leadership problems and improving leadership effectiveness, independent of traditional leadership competency models developed by the human resources community, or training programs rooted in complex industrial psychology or organizational behavior theories. Thus, we can use an existing Lean tool, one that reflects your actual workplace, for an entirely different purpose while remaining fully consistent with Lean principles and practices.

Traditional leadership competency models [6] suffer four major shortcomings:

- They are complex
- They are disconnected from the real world
- The desired competencies are assumed to be the correct ones
- The entire basis of competency models rests upon the view that behaviors lead to competencies.

Thus, changing leadership behaviors will lead to new leadership competencies which the organization desires in order to meet current and future business challenges. This has long been the approach taken by Lean trainers and consultants, as they have simply adopted ready-made tools developed long ago by the human resources community. However, seeking behavioral change in top company leaders without addressing their underlying beliefs about business will be ineffective.

Traditional leadership competency models assume the beliefs that executives possess are uniform, which is not the case. This can best be seen through the lens of value stream maps, which are real-world depictions of what goes on in a business every day.

Current and future state value stream maps are much simpler to understand than traditional leadership competency models or emotional intelligence constructs. In addition, the value stream maps reveal the existence of different belief systems among executives in conventionally-managed businesses compared to Lean businesses.

Instead of going from behavior to competency as traditional competency models do, the value stream maps show that we must back up one step and take into account managers' beliefs because they are not universally the same [7]. Figure 5-1 shows the progression from beliefs to behaviors to competencies found in value stream maps.

Figure 5-1

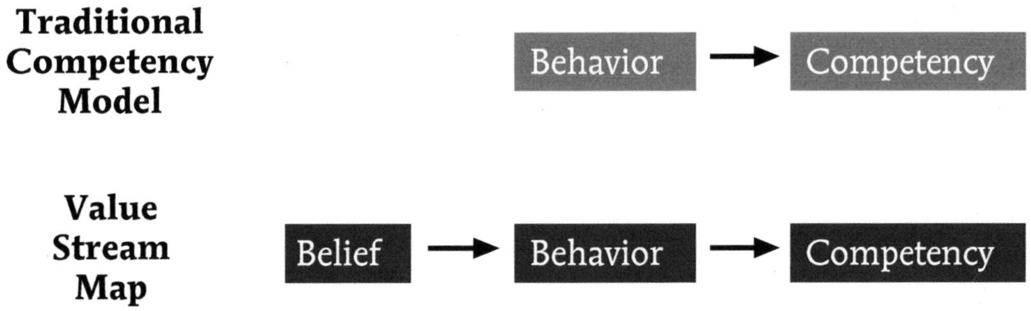

Traditional Competency Model   Behavior → Competency

Value Stream Map   Belief → Behavior → Competency

It is important to understand that Lean leaders value competencies rooted in Lean principles and practices, but they do not have any use for traditional leadership competency models [6].

Let's now look at an example of current and future state value stream maps and understand how they contain information encoded within them about leaders' beliefs, behaviors, and competencies [7]. We will use a manufacturing example, but the results will be exactly the same for service value stream maps.

Figure 5-2a shows the current state value stream map for a company that produces stamped and welded metal brackets in left-hand and right-hand configurations. It depicts the best known way of satisfying customer demand at the present time. It reflects the combined knowledge of everyone in the organization, and has the stamp of approval by top executives. Figure 5-2a includes the following information:

- Customer requirements communicated electronically as 90/60/30 day forecasts and daily orders
- Production control calculates weekly requirements using material requirementsplanning (MRP) software system and delivers a print-out of the schedule to each process
- Steel coil requirements communicated to the supplier via weekly fax
- Steel coils delivered twice per week by the supplier to meet a five-day supplyrequirement
- Five discrete processing steps (stamping, two welding, and two assembly) are used to produce brackets
- Stamping machine changeover time = 1 hour
- Each operation produces uncontrolled quantities of work-in-process independent of one another due to multi-point scheduling
- Average machine uptime = 93%
- Completed brackets are shipped to the customer once per day
- System lead-time = 23.5 days
- Processing time = 184 seconds

Two of the most telling pieces of information are the long lead-time, 23.5 days, and the short processing time, 184 seconds, which means that the company will have difficulty competing on the basis of time and invariably suffer from high costs and poor quality as well.

To support the current state, executives have to believe in various things about business, how to produce goods, and how to satisfy customer demand. Your assignment is to identify the leadership beliefs, behaviors, and competencies for the current state. Figure 5-2b contains two examples that show the progression from leadership beliefs to behaviors to competencies. Complete the remaining rows simply by looking at Figure 5-2a. You will need to think about management's beliefs regarding information from customers (top right), information to suppliers (top left), material deliveries (left side), information to production processes (middle), how brackets are made (bottom), scheduling, how work-in-process is managed, etc.

Figure 5-2a

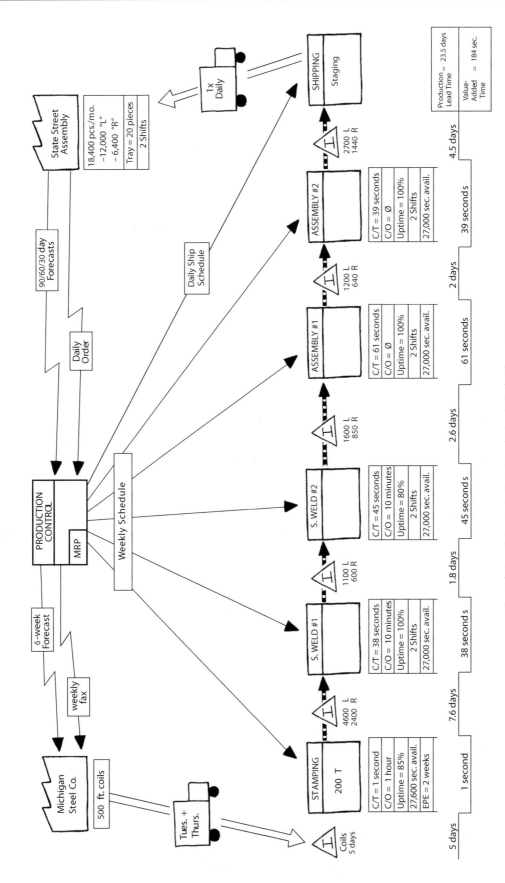

Copyright Lean Enterprise Institute (www.lean.org). Used with permission.

Figure 5-2b

Leadership Belief Something accepted as true.		**Leadership Behavior** Conduct based on beliefs.		**Leadership Competency** An established skill or capability.										
• Takes many steps to make a bracket		• Keep and improve each step • Add more steps if necessary		• Maintain status quo • Increase costs										
• Completed parts must wait until all parts are completed		• Drive people to work faster, plus re-schedule and expedite		• Maintain high costs and long lead times • Develop bad labor-management relations										

The picture that emerges is that current state beliefs lead to behaviors that result in *undesirable* competencies. Simply put, you get good at doing things that are bad for your customers and your company, employees, suppliers, and investors. No executive in the world would want to be known for maintaining the status quo, increasing costs, having long lead-times, or having bad relationships with employees. But that, and more, is exactly what current state value stream maps show.

Figure 5-3a shows the future state value stream map. It includes the following information:

- Customer requirements communicated electronically as 90/60/30 day forecasts and daily orders
- Production control issues daily orders to shipping department using inexpensive kanban (work instruction) card system
- Steel coil requirements communicated to supplier daily via computer
- Steel coil delivered daily by supplier to a "supermarket" (controlled inventory used to schedule work at an upstream process)
- Two discrete processing steps: one stamping operation with machine changeover time <10 minutes, and combined welding and assembly operations
- Quantity of brackets produced limited to the size of the supermarkets
- Average machine uptime = 100%
- Completed brackets are shipped to the customer once per day
- System lead-time = 4.5 days
- Processing time = 166 seconds

In this case, there is a large reduction in stamping machine changeover time and also the elimination of several queues by combining operations, which enables a much shorter system lead-time of 4.5 days (80% reduction). Operations have been combined resulting in 10% reduction in processing time, production is coordinated through the use of controlled inventories, and information is conveyed using simple kanban cards. The future state obviously represents a much more competitive position that the business and its customers will enjoy.

Your next assignment is to identify the leadership beliefs, behaviors, and competencies for the future state. Figure 5-3b contains two examples that show the progression from leadership beliefs to behaviors to competencies. Complete the remaining rows simply by looking at Figure 5-3a. Again, you will need to think about management's beliefs regarding information from customers (top right), information to suppliers (top left), material deliveries (left side), information to production areas (middle), scheduling, how brackets are made (bottom), how work-in-process is managed, etc.

Figure 5-3a

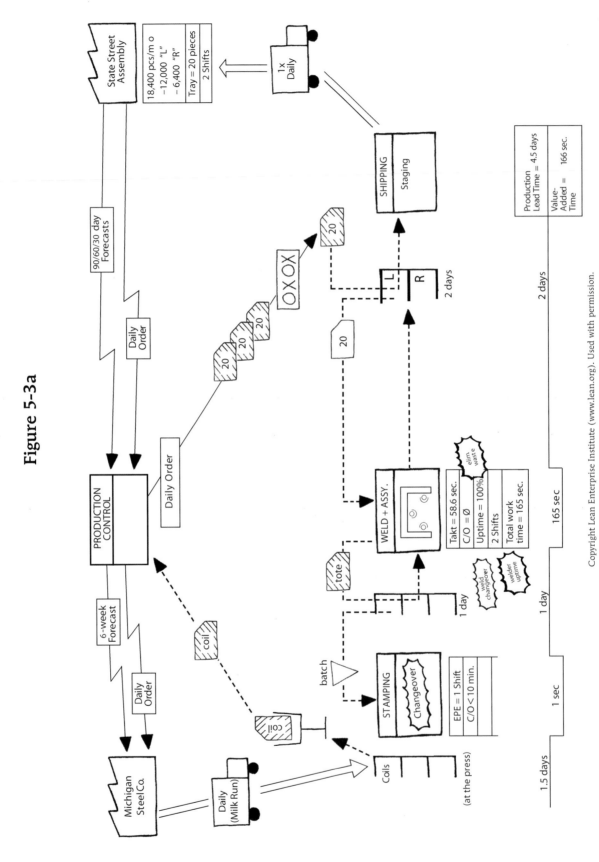

Copyright Lean Enterprise Institute (www.lean.org). Used with permission.

Figure 5-3b

Leadership Belief Something accepted as true.	Leadership Behavior Conduct based on beliefs.	Leadership Competency An established skill or capability.
• Brackets can be made in fewer steps • Completed parts do not have to wait until all parts are completed	• Question the process • Reduce number of steps • Engage people in simplifying work and improving processes	• Reduce lead-time • Reduce costs • Reduce costs and reduce lead times • Improve labor-management relations

The picture that emerges this time is completely different. The future state beliefs lead to behaviors that result in *desirable* competencies. Simply put, you get good at doing things that are good for your customers, your company, employees, suppliers, and investors. Every executive in the world wants their rhetoric to match up to the reality and wants to be known for being progressive and responsive, good at reducing costs and lead-times, and developing better relationships with employees and other stakeholders. That is exactly what the future state value stream maps show.

The answers to this exercise are shown on the next two pages.

Figure 5-2b Current State

Leadership Belief Something accepted as true.	Leadership Behavior Conduct based on beliefs.	Leadership Competency An established skill or capability.
• Many processing steps are needed • Add steps if needed • Two welding and two assembly operations are needed • Need 2 shifts to meet customer demand	• Don't question the process • Ignore improvement opportunities	• Maintain the status quo • Increase costs (current labor, material, space, and equipment expenses and future liabilities – e.g. pensions and healthcare) • Employ more people than needed (i.e. over-hire) • Increase lead-times
• Production Control (MRP) determines what to make, how much to make, when to make it.	• Don't question the process • Communicate requirements to people at every operation	• Cause confusion over what to make, how much to make, when to make it • Increase costs (over/under produce, software) • Create need for constant "firefighting" • Reward heroes
• Large amounts of WIP are needed to meet customer requirements • Inventories are an asset • Long LT can't be reduced • Stamping machine change-over time can not be reduced • Lower unit cost by increasing volume	• Accept batch-and-queue production method • Ignore queues • Don't question cause of long LT • Ignore improvement opportunities • Reduce number of set-ups	• Overproduction (to absorb costs) • Unresponsive to changing customer demand • Manage work-in-process and finished goods inventories • Increase costs (people, space and equipment to manage inventories) • Maintain the status quo
• Raw material unit cost reduced by increasing purchase volume • Can't change steel coil supplier's delivery terms	• Don't question the process • Ignore improvement opportunities • Maintain 5-day supply of steel coil	• Increase costs (raw material and overhead) • Manage raw material inventories
• Processes do not need to be connected to each other; each produces at own pace	• No effort made to connect individual processes	• Manage raw material, work-in-process, and finished goods inventories • Slow response to changes in customer demand
• I don't have to worry about what's going on in the factory; other people will take care of that	• Stay in office • Spend the day in meetings • Blame people when things go wrong	• No understanding of value-added and waste • Poor observation skills • Focus on the people, not the process

Figure 5-3b Future State

Leadership Belief Something accepted as true.	Leadership Behavior Conduct based on beliefs.	Leadership Competency An established skill or capability.
• Can make brackets with fewer steps • Welding and assembly operations can be combined • Need two shifts at current time; maybe can get to one shift	• Question the process • Support improvement opportunities • Identify value-added work, non-value added but necessary work, and waste	• Challenge the status quo • Cost reduction (current labor, material, space, and equipment expenses and future liabilities – e.g. pensions and healthcare) • Employ right number of people • Reduce lead-times
• Customer determines what to make, how much to make, when to make it – and transmit the information using simple kanban cards	• Question the process (go see) • Listen to customers • Communicate requirements to people at last operation (pull)	• Clarify what to make, how much to make, when to make it • Reduce costs (e.g. eliminate MRP cost) • Reduce or eliminate expediting • Reward people who improve processes
• Don't need large amounts of WIP to meet customer requirements • Inventories are waste • Lead-time can be reduced • Waste exists in every process • Stamping machine change-over time can be reduced • Short change-over times reduce unit cost	• Accept small lot production method • Support improvement opportunities • Increase number of quick set-ups • Question cause of long lead-time • Identify value-added work, non-value added but necessary work, and waste	• Responsive to changing customer needs • Produce to customer demand • Waste identification and elimination • Time-based competitiveness • Cost reduction (less inventory; less space and equipment needed to manage inventories) • Understand customer needs
• Steel coil supplier is a valuable resource that can better serve our needs • Buy only what is needed when needed	• Question the process • Support improvement opportunities	• Cost reduction (raw material and overhead) • Develop supplier relationships
• Processes need to be connected to each other; produce what is requested by downstream process	• Support efforts to connect individual processes	• Synchronize material and information flows • Fast response to changes in customer demand
• I have to understand what's going on in the factory to help ensure customer satisfaction	• Visit the shop floor frequently • Work with people to improve processes • Blame the process when things go wrong	• Understand value-added and waste • Strong observation skills • Focus on the process, not the people

So what is the significance of this?

> **Most executives who possess current state beliefs will never be able to achieve their business objectives, but they will try very hard to do so using value-destroying zero-sum mindsets and methods.**

On the other hand, the competencies that result from future state beliefs and behaviors are aligned with desired business outcomes, both stated and inferred. Further, future state beliefs enable better communication and greater depths of learning among managers and employees, which, in turn, will lead to improved competitiveness.

In addition, using value stream maps to improve leadership is much less expensive than traditional leadership training and development programs which do not link strongly to your actual business needs and circumstances.

Another way to comprehend the benefits of using value stream maps to improve leadership is as follows. Who would you rather compete against; leaders whose beliefs, behaviors, and competencies are rooted in the current state, or leaders whose beliefs, behaviors, and competencies reflect are rooted in the future state? There is no doubt you would rather compete against those leaders stuck in the current state. The question is; are you the one who is stuck in the current state?

The beliefs, behaviors, and competencies of Lean leaders are not limited to what can be deduced from future state value stream maps. There are over 30 additional key beliefs that Lean leaders possess that are different from the beliefs that executives of conventionally-managed business possess [8].

The only way to gain future state beliefs is by participating in kaizen and by studying and practicing Lean management, and applying your new knowledge in a consistent and disciplined manner. Most executives do not participate in kaizen, which means they never gain future state beliefs that are essential to have in order to lead a Lean transformation. That is why it is so important to become personally engaged in kaizen as a team member, not as a team leader.

After executives gain sufficient experience as team members, they could then become team leaders provided their roles as executive and team leader do not cause confusion among the workers. Also, executives should never lead kaizens in their area of responsibility due to obvious role conflicts.

The next chapter presents some of they key things that executives need to know about kaizen.

Chapter 5 – Self-Study
Write your responses in the space provided.

 Thinking

1. Based on the contents of Chapters 1-4, identify 10 additional beliefs that Lean leaders have that are different from the beliefs of non-Lean leaders.

-           •

-           •

-           •

-           •

-           •

2. Identify 10 problems that will occur if two or three members of the senior management team possess future state value stream map beliefs, behaviors, and competencies, while the remaining seven or eight members of the senior management team possess current state value stream map beliefs, behaviors, and competencies.

-           •

-           •

-           •

-           •

-           •

3. What do current state value stream maps tell you with regards to senior management's perception of time?

4. What do current state value stream maps tell you with regards to senior management's perception of money?

5. What do current state value stream maps tell you with regards to senior management's views of the markets they serve and of competition?

6. Has your company's past leadership development programs delivered tangible, bottom-line benefits? If not, why not?

7. In what ways do current state value stream maps reflect the zero-sum thinking that is typically possessed by executives.

Doing

1. Identify the senior management team's beliefs, behaviors, and competencies using current state value stream maps from your company for an important activity in finance.

2. Identify the senior management team's beliefs, behaviors, and competencies using current state value stream maps from your company for an important activity in sales or marketing.

3. Identify the senior management team's beliefs, behaviors, and competencies using current state value stream maps from your company for an important activity in human resources.

4. Identify the senior management team's beliefs, behaviors, and competencies using current state value stream maps from your company for an important activity in legal.

5. Identify the senior management team's beliefs, behaviors, and competencies using current state value stream maps from your company for an important activity in new product development.

6. How will you integrate current and future state value stream maps into executive performance appraisal, base pay and incentive compensation, and in promotion processes?

Action Plan*

Who	Will Do What	By When

* Make sure you do not delegate that which only you should do.

Commit These to Memory
- Lean leadership beliefs are completely different than the beliefs held by leaders who practice conventional management.
- Beliefs lead to behaviors, which, in turn, result in competencies that can either be good or bad.
- Lean leadership beliefs are learned by participating in kaizen and by studying and practicing Lean management.
- Competencies that result from future state beliefs and behaviors are aligned with desired business outcomes.

6

What Executives Need to Know About Kaizen

Chapter Highlights
• How to create a Lean culture
• Understand intent and meaning of kaizen
• Importance of executive participation in kaizen

One of the most highly sought-after characteristics of a Lean enterprise is its culture. The word culture means the beliefs and assumptions that guide people's thinking and decision making. If you change your beliefs you will begin to change the culture of your company. But be fore-warned: Lean culture does not stick by itself. You can practice Lean management for 30 years, but the culture will fade away within two or three years if Lean principles and practices are no longer used. It is analogous to taking a long break from playing a musical instrument: take two or three years off from playing piano and your knowledge and skills will deteriorate significantly.

It takes ongoing inputs of Lean practice to maintain and grow the Lean culture. The primary route to gaining a Lean culture is through participation in kaizen [1-4]. If executives do not participate in kaizen, then the Lean culture will not emerge. Recall from Chapter 1 that the literal translation of kaizen is:

> **"Change for the better"**
> *in a multilateral context.*

Also recall that understanding kaizen more narrowly as "continuous improvement" invites confusion and often leads to the misapplication of kaizen in a unilateral, or zero-sum context, such as laying people off as a result of productivity improvement. Laying people off as a result of kaizen is inconsistent with the "Respect for People" principle. Employees must not fear kaizen. Therefore,

> **Employees whose job is impacted by kaizen will be re-deployed to work in other parts of the company.**

You must re-deploy your people and grow sales. And the way you re-deploy people matters: it must be done in a manner that is consistent with the "Respect for People" principle. Failure to do so will result in fake kaizen. For example, workers who are re-deployed must not suffer a loss in pay. Also, supervisors will be tempted to re-deploy the weakest team members, but should instead re-deploy the best team members because they will be better able to use their new knowledge and skills for successful re-deployment.

Kaizen is typically practiced by executives in a manner that is inconsistent with the "Respect for People" principle, so it is not surprising that employees, supervisors, and mid-level managers will resist participating in kaizen or undermine kaizens and cause them to fail. This is a painfully obvious cause-and-effect that nearly every executive chooses to ignore. Executives must never ignore this cause-and-effect and must get involved in reversing people's negative perceptions of kaizen. This task will be much easier for executives who participate in kaizen and also understand the deeper meanings of kaizen.

So what is kaizen? Kaizen is a process led by an experienced facilitator called a "sensei" (teacher) who teaches a cross-functional team of people how to identify and eliminate waste, unevenness, and unreasonableness, so that people can focus their efforts on value-added work. Kaizen facilitated correctly results in the simultaneous achievement of several favorable outcomes, including improved productivity, quality, and working conditions; reduced lead-time; lower costs; and improved communication and morale. Kaizen is a process for learning and should be fun and engaging. If not, then kaizen is being practiced incorrectly.

Learning is a very important aspect of Lean management. Kaizen plays a key role in teaching people how to:

- Recognize a problem
- Analyze a problem quickly
- Identify countermeasures
- Implement countermeasures
- Measure and evaluate results

Recall the current state value stream map shown in Figure 5-2a. It proves that people are not good at doing these five things – despite what they may say or think.

It is correct to say "kaizen;" it is incorrect to say "kaizen event," "kaizen blitz," "kaizen project," or "kaizen burst." Referring to kaizen as an "event" leads people to think they can be successful doing three or four kaizens per year, when in fact kaizen is a daily activity. Referring to kaizen as a "blitz" suggests to people that something bad may happen to them. Referring to kaizen as a "project" is a turnoff. Who wants yet another project? "Kaizen burst" is the name of a symbol used in value stream mapping; it is not the name of an activity. Therefore, just say "kaizen."

Kaizen must be practiced using the following three principles [5]:

> **Process and Results**
> **Systems Focus**
> **Non-blaming, Non-judgmental**

"Process and results" is intended to inform executives that process *and* results matter. Most executives are results-focused and do not care about process, which explains why errors are endlessly repeated. This will be a big shift, as most executives are poor at thinking in terms of processes.

"Systems focus" is intended to inform executives that the purpose of kaizen is to improve the entire business system. In contrast, leaders of conventionally-managed businesses focus on making isolated improvements within a given department or functional area, typically at the expense of some other department or functional area. Kaizen that is good for one part of the business but bad for an upstream or downstream process is unilateral kaizen, which is inconsistent with both the "Continuous Improvement" and "Respect for People" principles. Kaizen must be multilateral; what is good for one part of the business must also be good for upstream and downstream processes.

"Non-blaming, non-judgmental" is intended to inform executives that people will not participate in kaizen if they are blamed for past mistakes or poor outcomes. Blaming people or being judgmental is inconsistent with the "Respect for People" principle.

Failure to employ these principles will lead to poor results and people's willingness to participate in kaizen will soon end.

The next question is: Who participates in kaizen? The answer is: *Everyone* participates in kaizen – from the chief executive officer to the lowest levels of the organization. Kaizen teams are comprised of cross-functional groups of people. They include people from the process which is the subject of the kaizen, as well as people from upstream and downstream processes. They also include people who may be far removed from the process. Everyone in every department participates, including legal, finance, human resources, design, corporate communications, etc. It is not necessary for every team member to have general or detailed knowledge of the process. If fact, some should have no knowledge of the process because they will look at it from fresh perspectives.

While there are many types of kaizen, these are the four major types:

Individual	**Daily**
Suggestion system	**Weekly**
Small team	**1/2 to 2 days**
Large team	**3-5 days or more**

Thus, kaizen ranges from an individual daily activity to a large cross-functional team activity. Large teams spend one to two days collecting data and facts in preparation for the kaizen. Large companies that are committed to Lean management typically have several large team kaizens every week, dozens or hundreds of small team kaizens every day, as well as daily individual efforts to eliminate waste, unevenness, and unreasonableness.

Executive participation in large team kaizens at the onset of a Lean transformation would be at least monthly and may perhaps taper off to six times a year after the first year and then settling to four times per year a few years later. Every employee, regardless of department or level, should participate in one to three large team kaizens per year, as well as numerous small team and individual kaizens. Kaizen practiced every day serves as a countermeasure against the re-introduction of conventional management thinking and practice into the organization

Participation on large or small team kaizens is not a part-time activity:

> **Team members must be committed to the kaizen for its duration, including the CEO, president, vice presidents, etc.**

Executives should delegate all of their work to others so they can give their undivided attention for the duration of the kaizen.

Common kaizen errors include:

- Scope of the kaizen is too large.
- The company does too few kaizens.
- Team members dictate to the facilitator what they plan to do.
- Management establishes kaizen improvement targets, thus disempowering the team to learn and establish its own targets. The kaizen facilitator has the sole responsibility to adjust the team's targets up or down. Management sets company targets, not individual kaizen targets.
- Management criticizes or second-guesses the team, disempowering the team and ruining its learning experience.
- Management steers or politicizes the kaizen team, which is inconsistent with both the "Continuous Improvement" and "Respect for People" principles.
- Executives become engaged in kaizen as team leaders without sufficient prior experience as team members. This causes confusion among workers regarding the executive's role –

is the executive a company leader or kaizen team leader during kaizen?

- Management agrees to support kaizen on a pilot basis, signaling skepticism or lack of confidence in the kaizen process or in the team members.

Senior management must do the following:

- Advocate kaizen
- Participate in kaizen
- Attend daily kaizen close-out meetings to show support and respect for the team members, as well as learn, share, and plan
- Practice the three principles of kaizen
- Budget for kaizen
- Identify kaizen opportunities
- Select cross-functional team members
- Support the teams

Executive must be aware that small errors in their understanding and practice of kaizen will lead to poor results and many problems.

In summary, kaizen is much more than just process improvement or cost reduction. Kaizen done correctly offers numerous benefits including:

- Teaches people how to see opportunities
- Teaches people how to think
- A process for learning
- Improves information flow
- Humanizes the workplace
- Creates a culture that asks, "Why?"
- Drives innovation
- Reduces barriers to interaction among people
- Improves people's understanding of the work
- Helps identify future leaders
- Changes people's beliefs

Kaizen makes you smarter, faster – but only if you do it right.

Chapter 6 – Self-Study
Write your responses in the space provided.

 Thinking

1. Describe why small daily improvements are preferable to intermittent large improvements.

2. Employees and line managers dislike kaizens for many different reasons. Some dislike Japanese words, others think the boss does not really care about improvement, most fear they will lose their job, while others think kaizen is a paperwork exercise. Describe several ways to can gain acceptance for kaizen among your employees and line managers when they possess such diverse negative views.

3. Kaizen helps eliminate difficult work and improve communication and morale. How could kaizen be practiced so that it would fail to achieve these favorable outcomes?

4. Identify 10 ways in which kaizen helps to humanize the workplace.

-
-
-
-
-

-
-
-
-
-

5. Identify five errors in decision making that you think kaizen could help eliminate.

-
-
-
-
-

6. What are the leadership beliefs that support the daily practice of kaizen?

Doing

1. Identify three large team kaizens you will participate in the coming six months.

Action Plan*

Kaizen	Date
1.	
2.	
3.	

* Make sure you do not delegate that which only you should do.

Commit These to Memory

- Kaizen means "change for the better," in a multilateral context.
- The three principles of kaizen are process and results, systems focus, and non-blaming, non-judgmental.
- Every executive, every manager, and every associate participates in kaizen.
- Employees whose jobs are impacted by kaizen will be re-deployed to work in other parts of the company at no loss of pay.
- Small errors in executives' understanding and practice of kaizen will lead to poor results and many problems.
- Kaizen makes you smarter, faster – but only if you do it right.

7

Standardized Work for Executive Leadership

Chapter Highlights
• Avoiding errors in executive decision making • The importance of non-zero-sum business principles • Standard skill set for executives

Daily reading of *The Wall Street Journal* tells an interesting story of the common errors made by senior managers – most of which are the result of deeply ingrained, zero-sum thinking. These errors are made by executives with advanced degrees and who typically have decades of business experience, yet are often exactly the same errors as those made by executives over 100 years ago. This should compel us to ask: "Why are these errors repeated?"

It is fair to say that most executives possess a casual view of errors based on how they attempt to correct errors. It is usually at the symptom level rather than at the root cause, and they often blame other people, external conditions, or events for having caused the errors. While executives are often trained in root cause analysis, it is extremely rare to find any who actually use the root cause analysis tools they were taught for the types of problems that they encounter.

Another reason why top leaders repeat errors is because there are no standards, or very poor standards, for the types of work they do – principally strategy, planning, and decision making versus the daily tasks of lower-level leaders [1]. Most executives do not perform their daily work according to standardized work as do lower-level workers in manufacturing [2-5], and more recently in office work such as purchasing, engineering, new product development, etc. Leaders often tell workers there are many benefits to standardized work; fewer errors, stability, making abnormalities visible, clarifying expectations, simplifying training of new personnel, and creating a reference point from which to continuously improve, but they do not consider how standardized work might apply to their jobs.

Instead, executives perform their work in accordance with procedures that often lack details of how to actually do the work, and of course they are often mired in time-consuming firefights. There is a common perception among executives that their duties are so widely varied from one day to the next that the application of standardized work to their activities is impossible. However, senior managers, like most office workers, think their entire workday is highly varied because that is what they remember most. In fact, carefully observing executives at work reveals that only some of their activities vary significantly from one day to the next.

The cause of variation in leaders' workday can often be traced to inconsistencies in decision making and incorrect decisions, which introduce new errors and other forms of variability. Since much of an executive's work is decision making, processes for decision making that lack standards can be inefficient and costly. Top leaders may inadvertently create much of the variation that they encounter. Executives who rationalize the variation they experience as "just the way things are" introduce barriers to the consideration of new ideas that might reduce variation and make their jobs easier to do and more enjoyable.

Another thing to consider is that executives commonly claim there is a shortage of qualified leaders. This statement indicates that, in their view, leadership is a specialized activity. Historically, specialization has tended towards standardization in the case of manual labor [6, 7] and some types of office work. The question is, can standardized work be applied to the work that executives do?

If so, standardization could help alleviate leadership shortages and reduce the total cost of leadership, inclusive of compensation and benefits, the cost of common errors that leaders make, etc. Standardized work will also help avoid backslide, make it easier to train future Lean leaders, and promote creativity. Executives who are open to the concept of standardized work applied to their activities will send a clear message that they are serious about participating in continuous improvement and avoiding errors.

It is obvious that not every aspect of a leader's duties can or should be standardized. Further, the intent of standardized work is not to undercut creativity, to carelessly force conformance of leadership to a process, or to suggest a "one best way" to do the job. However, a substantial portion of an executive's daily work activities could be standardized, and this would have wide-ranging benefits to an organization and its key stakeholders. Executives who accept standardized work will enjoy substantial long-term benefits, especially with its consistent application over generations of managers. So how do you do it?

Let's first look at the definition of standardized work for operators, published by the Lean Enterprise Institute [8]:

"Establishing precise procedures for each operator's work in a production process, based on three elements:

1. **Takt time, which is the rate at which products must be made in a process to meet customer demand.**
2. **The precise work sequence in which an operator performs tasks within takt time.**
3. **The standard inventory, including units in machines, required to keep the process operating smoothly.**

Standardized work, once established..., is the object of continuous improvement through kaizen."

This definition of standardized work pertains to the work of shop-floor associates in a manufacturing business, and is obviously not suitable for executives. But the concept of standardized work can be applied to the work executives do in a similar fashion [9].

The idea is to realize improvement by eliminating the types of errors that leaders commonly make. While the diligent use of formal root cause analysis tools will be necessary, so too will be the establishment of standardized work to make processes such as decision making more efficient and less costly. If standardized work is important enough to be applied at the shop-floor level to avoid errors costing anywhere from a few dollars to several thousand dollars or perhaps more, then it certainly makes sense to apply standardized work to executives' work to avoid more expensive financial and non-financial errors, perhaps even up to those that lead to forced sale, reorganization under bankruptcy code, or liquidation.

So what does standardized work for executives look like? We can start by modifying the previous definition as follows:

> "Establishing a precise framework for each leader's work in business processes, based on three elements:
>
> 1. A definition of leadership that satisfies the needs of internal and external customers.
> 2. A precise description of non-zero-sum business principles that leaders use to perform their work.
> 3. A standard skill set to keep business processes operating smoothly.
>
> Standardized work, once established, is the object of continuous improvement through kaizen."

The first element of standardized work for executives is a definition of leadership. We will use the definition given in Chapter 3.

> **Beliefs, behaviors, and competencies that demonstrate respect for people, motivate people, improve business conditions, minimize or eliminate organizational politics, ensure effective utilization of resources, and eliminate confusion and rework.**

The second element of standardized work is a description of non-zero-sum business principles which leaders can use to perform their work. Rather than create from scratch the second element of standardized work, we can simply use the Caux Round Table *Principles for Business* as the standardized description of multilateral business principles (see Appendix II):

The Caux Round Table *Principles for Business* is a practical, real-world expression of principled business behavior crafted by CEO-level business leaders in 1994. It is an explicit description of the types of relationships that business executives should want to seek with their key stakeholders – customers, employees, suppliers, investors, communities, and competitors – and consists of seven general principles and six stakeholder principles.

The *Principles for Business* are essential for driving executives away from zero-sum management thinking and practices, where winners gain at the expense of losers, to non-zero-sum [10]. Success with Lean management requires leaders to understand and practice non-zero-sum management thinking and practices, where all parties share in the benefits.

The third element of standardized work is a standard skill set to keep business processes operating smoothly. The formulation of a skill set for executives will differ from how the term is applied to factory or office worker activities. In this case, the term "skill set" is a bit broader and consists of the mindsets, behaviors, and skills that will help keep business processes operating smoothly. It is as follows:

- Customer First – Recognizing the importance of the customer to business continuity and satisfying their ever-changing needs.
- Process and Results – Avoiding the dysfunctional "results are the only thing that matter" view that is prevalent among executives.
- Developing People – Commitment to developing associates and to create future leaders through significant cross-functional work experience.

- Quantitative plus Qualitative – Balance quantitative and qualitative information to make correct decisions, rather than focusing almost exclusively on the numbers.
- Go See / Get Hands Dirty – Willingness to go to the source; to engage people in a non-blaming, non-judgmental way; comfortable doing front-line value-adding work periodically as a way to learn and improve.
- PDCA Cycle – Uses Plan-Do-Check-Act cycle for continuous improvement.
- Root Cause Analysis – Uses simple root cause analysis tools to better understand the source of problems and identify countermeasures.
- Time Consciousness – Responsiveness to problems and knowing when to respond to opportunities.
- Stakeholders as Resources, Not Costs – Possesses positive view that stakeholders are resources to the enterprise.
- Technology to Help People – Understands role of technology to help people and support business processes, not as a means to eliminate people.
- Sharing – Shares wealth among various stakeholders to create new opportunities and drive business growth.

Figure 7-1 shows the complete description of standardized work for executives that they should use in most daily activities, and especially for strategy, planning, and decision making:

Figure 7-1

Establishing a precise framework for each leader's work in business processes, based on three elements:	
1. A definition of leadership that satisfies the needs of internal and external customers.	Beliefs, behaviors, and competencies that demonstrate respect for people, motivate people, improve business conditions, minimize or eliminate organizational politics, ensure effective utilization of resources, and eliminate confusion and rework.
2. A precise description of non-zero-sum business principles that leaders use to perform their work.	Caux Round Table *Principles for Business* • Seven General Principles • Six Stakeholder Principles
3. A standard skill set to keep business processes operating smoothly.	Customer First; Process and Results; Developing People; Quantitative plus Qualitative; Go See / Get Hands Dirty; PDCA Cycle; Root Cause Analysis; Time Consciousness; Stakeholders as Resources, Not Costs; Technology to Help People; Sharing
Standardized work, once established, is the object of continuous improvement through kaizen.	

The benefits of standardized work for executive leadership include:

- Documentation of current leadership process
- Reduction in variability (fewer errors) in leadership activities
- Less backslide in Lean transformations
- Simplified training of new leaders and flexibility in staffing
- Establish a baseline for improvement

The standardized work shown in Figure 7-1 will yield better long-term results because it is specific and comprehensive, yet also relatively simple and concise. Daily use of standardized work will improve the efficiency and effectiveness of leadership decision making and develop leadership capabilities much in the same way that daily practice improves a musician's efficiency and capabilities.

Once standardized work is established, the next step is to perform the work to the standard, measure the results, and make corrections. Appropriate rewards will have to be established for executives who adhere to standardized work and meaningful corrections devised by the leadership team in advance for those who do not.

Ultimately, the effectiveness of standardized work shown in Figure 7-1 depends upon whether or not executives will individually and collectively contribute to ensuring the survival of standardized work over generations of leaders. This should be a key responsibility of the CEO and board of directors.

Chapter 7 – Self-Study
Write your responses in the space provided.

 Thinking

1. Identify 10 types of executive decision making errors that standardized work for executives will help eliminate.

-
-
-
-
-
-
-
-
-
-

2. Identify your top five personal barriers that prevent implementing standardized work for executives (Figure 7-1) and identify two practical countermeasures for each barrier.

Barrier	Rationale	Countermeasure

3. Identify the top five organizational barriers that prevent implementing standardized work for executives (Figure 7-1) and identify two practical countermeasures for each barrier.

Barrier	Rationale	Countermeasure

4. Describe how corporate purpose links to standardized work for executive leadership.

5. What circumstances might arise that would require standardized work for executive leadership to become the subject of continuous improvement?

6. What circumstances might arise where standardized work for executive leadership should not be changed?

7. Describe how you think employees who must adhere to standardized work will respond when they learn that the executive team will conduct most of its work according to standardized work.

8. Read the Caux Round Table *Principles for Business* in the Appendix II. Identify where you feel your company is inconsistent with the *Principles for Business* for each of the following categories: "General Principles" (Section 2, Principles 1-7) and "Stakeholder Principles" (Section 3, Customers, Employees, Owners/Investors, etc.). Put a checkmark in the middle column of the table below where you feel there is one or more occurrence of inconsistency, and provide a short rationale or example.

Inconsistent with CRT *Principles for Business*

	Inconsistent	Brief Rationale or Example
General Principles		
• Principle 1. The Responsibilities Of Businesses		
• Principle 2. The Economic and Social Impact of Business		
• Principle 3. Business Behavior		
• Principle 4. Respect for Rules		
• Principle 5. Support for Multilateral Trade		
• Principle 6. Respect for the Environment		
• Principle 7. Avoidance of Illicit Operations		
Stakeholder Principles		
• Customers		
• Employees		
• Owners / Investors		
• Suppliers		
• Competitors		
• Communities		

The radar chart below shows the aggregate results from a survey of nearly 250 independent contributors, supervisors, managers, and executives regarding their perceptions of their organizations' performance relative to the *Principles for Business*.

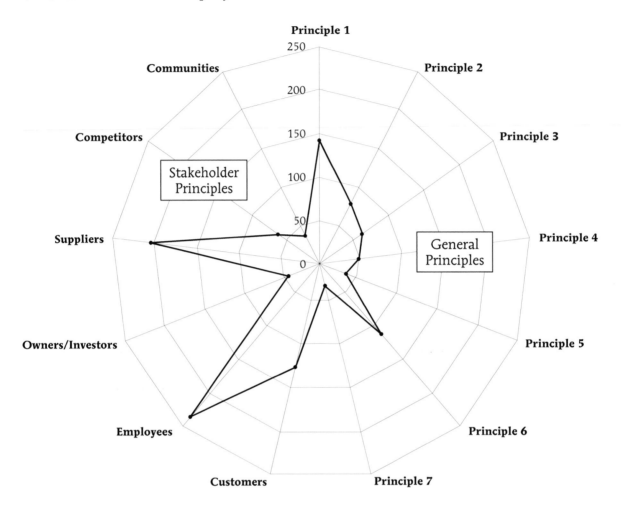

The chart is interpreted as follows: data points further away from the center indicate a perception of inconsistency between their company's performance and the *Principles for Business*, whereas data points near the center indicate a perception of consistency. If a company was consistent with the Caux Round Table *Principles for Business*, then the data would appear as a small circle located close to the center.

a) Explain any inconsistency that exists between your perceptions of your company's performance relative to the *Principles for Business* and that shown in the radar chart, which also likely reflects the perception of employees in your company.

b) The radar chart shows large variances, or a lack of balance. There is a perception that company executives strongly favor some stakeholders over others (left side of chart), and are more responsive to some of the General Principles but not to others (right side of chart). What types of problems will this lack of balance cause?

c) In the radar chart, there is a perception that executives are consistent with the *Principles for Business* with respect to investors' interests. What data contained in the chart clearly refute this perception?

d) What strategic problems will your company face if employees' and suppliers' interests are so strongly marginalized?

e) What day-to-day practical problems will you face daily as a leader if employees' interests are so strongly marginalized?

Doing

1. Identify which of the 11 items listed in the standard skill set you need to better understand and practice, and create an action plan.

Action Plan*

I Will Do What	By When

* Make sure you do not delegate that which only you should do.

2. What concrete steps can the leadership team take to address the waste, unevenness, and unreasonableness that will result from the lack of balance shown in the radar chart?

Who	Does What	By When

* Make sure you do not delegate that which only you should do.

3. Create an action plan for implementing standardized work for executive leadership (Figure 7-1).

Action Plan*

Who	Does What	By When

Make sure you do not delegate that which only you should do.

4. Establish rewards for executives who adhere to standardized work and determine meaningful corrections for those who do not, consistent with the "Continuous Improvement" and "Respect for People" principles.

Action Plan*

Who	Does What	By When

Make sure you do not delegate that which only you should do.

5. How will standardized work be incorporated into executive performance appraisal, base pay and incentive compensation, and in promotion processes?

Action Plan*

Who	Does What	By When

Make sure you do not delegate that which only you should do.

Commit These to Memory

- Lean organizations must have non-zero-sum business principles that are explicit.
- Business principles should compliment the statement of corporate purpose.
- Marginalizing the interests of key stakeholders creates waste, unevenness, and unreasonableness.
- Standardized work for executive leadership is a practical countermeasure to minimize or prevent errors made by executives.

8

Fifty Errors to Avoid

Chapter Highlights

- Understand common Lean transformation errors
- How errors disrupt Lean transformation efforts
- How to avoid common errors

The roots of Lean management date back to the Scientific Management era of the mid-1880s and early 1900s, when the first modern system of industrial management was developed by Frederick W. Taylor and his associates [1, 2]. Executives seeking to implement Scientific Management, and Lean management after that, have always struggled much more than needed, resulting in uneven outcomes. Unfortunately, there has been remarkable consistency in the errors made by thousands of executives from the late 1800s to the present [3].

Executives often demand flawless execution from employees in the performance of their work. But when it comes to Lean transformations, execution by executives is almost always highly flawed. Large and even small errors in executives' understanding and practice of Lean management will rapidly undermine everyone's Lean efforts. Errors, especially the common ones, must be sharply minimized or not made at all if executives wish to avoid problems and unfavorable outcomes.

Below are 50 common errors that executives make when implementing Lean management, but which are easy to avoid. Most of these errors are, to use the tennis term, "unforced errors."

> **The errors listed below that are denoted with a single asterisk have been repeated for 100 years or more, all the way back to back to the era of Scientific Management, while the errors denoted with a double asterisk have been repeated for over 30 years.**

1. Incorrectly characterizing the Lean management system.*

Characterizing Lean management as an "initiative," a "program," or a "regimen" gives people the impression that Lean is an activity that will soon pass. Characterizing Lean as a "manufacturing thing" signals to executives in charge of engineering, human resources, finance, sales, legal, information technology, etc., that they do not have to bother learning Lean principles and practices.

2. Incorrectly characterizing kaizen.**

Characterizing kaizen as an "event," "blitz," "project," or "burst" carries connotations that do not accurately portray the meaning or intent of kaizen [4]. Remember, the literal meaning of the word kaizen is "change for the better," in a multilateral context. That means the change must be good for all stakeholders. For example, a change that is good for the company or its shareholders but bad for employees or suppliers is not kaizen. A change that is good for engineering but bad for manufacturing or sales is not kaizen.

3. Doing kaizen without the three principles of kaizen.**

Kaizen without the application of these three principles is not kaizen [5]:
- Process and results
- Systems focus (not silo focus)
- Non-blaming, non-judgmental

Kaizen done correctly helps improve cooperation, communication, and enthusiasm for work.

4. Confusing terms used in Lean management with terms used in conventional management.**

Standardized work is correct, while work standards has a different meaning and is used for different purposes [6]. Target cost is correct, while cost targets has a different meaning and is used for different purposes [7].

5. Confusing the types of waste.**

There are eight wastes; defects, transportation, overproduction, waiting, processing, movement, inventory [8], and behaviors [9]. The waste of processing is commonly misunderstood as overprocessing. The waste is processing itself, not overprocessing, because it challenges people to ask if the entire process can be eliminated rather than just a part of the process.

6. Thinking that your conception of teamwork is the same as teamwork in a Lean environment.*

We all use the same word, but teamwork in a conventionally-managed business is very different than in a Lean business that lives by the principles "Continuous Improvement" and "Respect for People." In conventional management teamwork is often forced, political, and zero-sum in its orientation. In a Lean environment teamwork is natural, harmonious, and non-zero-sum in its orientation.

7. Confusing Lean management principles.**

"Continuous Improvement" and "Respect for People" is correct, "Just-In-Time" and "Respect for People" is incorrect [10]. This mixes up the pillars of The Toyota Way ("Continuous Improvement" and "Respect for People") [11] with the pillars of the Toyota Production System ("Just-In-Time" and "Autonomation") [8].

8. Not knowing the difference between REAL Lean and Fake or Imitation Lean.*

REAL Lean is the non-zero-sum application of both Lean principles, "Continuous Improvement" and "Respect for People." Fake or imitation Lean is the zero-sum application of the Lean principle, "Continuous Improvement" only. Fake Lean is narrowly focused on the tools of continuous improvement. The slogan "flawless execution," for example, supports Fake Lean because it cuts off people's desire to try new things and learn.

9. Mistaking a little Lean knowledge for a lot of Lean knowledge.*

You can't read the first 100 pages of *Lean Thinking* [12] and know Lean management.

10. Adding new Lean knowledge without eliminating old conventional management knowledge.*

New Lean knowledge must displace old knowledge and practices that are inconsistent with Lean.

11. Assuming you can become good at Lean management without having to practice every day.*

Proficiency in any endeavor requires enduring commitment to daily practice [4, 13].

12. Applying zero-sum thinking and habits in the application of Lean.*

Lean is a non-zero-sum system of management. Zero-sum thinking must be eliminated.

13. Thinking the leadership skills that got you to where you are will work in a Lean environment.*

The beliefs, behaviors, and competencies of leaders skilled in the Lean management system are completely different than those possessed by managers skilled in conventional management practices [14, 15].

14. Blaming middle managers for resisting Lean.*

You must resist the temptation to blame people. When problems occur, do root cause analysis to understand the true nature of the problem. The first rule in performing root cause analysis is to focus on the process, not on the people. Root cause analysis works only if it used in a no-blame environment.

15. Thinking that blame is helpful.*

Blame is waste; it adds cost but does not add value and can be eliminated [9].

16. Not acknowledging the existence of behavioral waste.**

Many people characterize the eighth waste as the "waste of creativity," "underutilizing worker talents," or "waste of people." Do a root cause analysis of why creativity, talents, or people are wasted, and you will see that the root cause is behavioral waste by members of the executive team [9].

17. Thinking that books on Lean management are theory.*

People often characterize books as theory, even when the author's stated focus is actual practice. The best books on Lean management [16] present ideas and practices grounded in the reality that zero-sum thinking leads to bad outcomes and that non-zero-sum thinking leads to better outcomes. Most executives operate under the theory that zero-sum thinking and actions have no negative consequences and have no costs. That is a fundamentally flawed theory [17].

18. Failing to recognize that the core competency concept is incompatible with Lean thinking.**

The core competency concept [18] is rooted in the results-oriented thinking patterns of conventional management practice, with little or no concern about business processes. Managers who subscribe to the core competencies concept usually end up outsourcing work that is not important to them, but is often very important to their customers. However, they don't know this because they don't have a good grasp of the customer's perception of value. Value stream maps tell you what you must do well, even if it is not a core competency.

19. Denying the existence of stakeholders.*

In bad times, executives typically call upon their stakeholders – employees, suppliers, customers, investors, communities, and sometimes even competitors – to help bail out the company. Why not instead recognize the existence of stakeholders in good times and work with them in a non-zero-sum fashion? This would be an effective countermeasure for avoiding bad times.

20. Operating a business without a purpose.*

Most companies do not have an explicit corporate purpose. Executives need to determine their company's corporate purpose. If you come up with a zero-sum based corporate purpose, or something like "our corporate purpose is to make money," you get an "F" and must start over. Hint: go find and study Toyota's corporate purpose [19].

21. Adopting Lean but not changing performance measurement metrics.*

This is simply a recipe for failure. All metrics currently in use need to be critically examined. Do they create or perpetuate waste, unevenness, or unreasonableness? If so, then eliminate them or de-emphasize their meaning and use within your organization [20].

22. Remaining fixated on unit costs and not understanding total costs.*

Senior managers typically do not understand the total cost of a purchase, just purchase price. They use purchasing tools that are inconsistent with Lean principles and practices such as economic order quantities and reverse auctions [21]. Price-based metrics such as purchase price variance (PPV) promote destructive zero-sum power-based bargaining with suppliers [22]. This makes it very difficult to engage in collaborative efforts with suppliers to identify and correct problems [23].

23. Remaining fixated on finding new tools to help correct current business problems.*

Tools feed management's perceived need for short-term solutions to problems. But have you noticed how tools are not really getting you anywhere? That's because everyone is using the same tools, so nobody gains much of an advantage. Also, reliance on tools helps managers avoid the deep and wide changes needed to faithfully serve buyers' markets. Tools used in the absence of corporate purpose and business principles are hurting you much more than they are helping you.

24. Confusion over who is the end-use customer.*

Many executives think Wall Street is their customer. That is wrong, except for the case of an initial or secondary public offering of stock. Otherwise, the source of your cash flow is your customers. Your end-use customers may or may not be sources of cash flow. Regardless, you better know who they are and what their value proposition is [12].

25. Not establishing a no-blame policy.*

Establishing a no-blame policy is easy. Making a no-blame policy come to life every day is the responsibility of all executives [24].

26. Not establishing a qualified job guarantee.*

Executives have to make it safe for people to change. If they do not do this, then people will not participate in kaizen. They need to guarantee employees that they will not become unemployed because of kaizen. However, by doing this they are not guaranteeing people a job for life. Executives should establish the following policy: "No associate shall be subject to layoff as a direct result of kaizen or other activity designed to improve business processes. Nothing shall restrict the rights of the company to adjust its workforce in response to business conditions" [24].

27. Poor ability to process non-quantitative information.*

Most top executives are strong with numbers, particularly financial numbers, but are weak at processing non-quantitative information. The common view is that having numerical control of a business represents the peak of management capability [25]. However, Lean leaders prefer to have process control as the input, which leads to numerical (financial) control as the output. They also prefer to have human intelligence control the system rather than have an unintelligent (financial or computer) system control the people. Numerical control can easily undercut human-centered Lean management, while only humans can include important intangible factors in decision making. Lean leaders are good at processing quantitative and non-quantitative information. They know that just because you can't put something into a financial spreadsheet doesn't mean it is not real.

28. Poor ability to comprehend cause-and-effect.*

If squeezing suppliers to obtain lower unit prices on purchased goods and services makes them mad, isn't it obvious they will find a way to get even and charge you a higher price when the opportunity to do so arises? Squeezing pay and benefits makes employees mad. Isn't it obvious they will find ways to get even? These are two of dozens of examples of how executives can marginalize the interests of key stakeholders. These actions have an effect similar to a chemical depressant in that they slow down response time to changing business conditions. They also lead to opportunistic behaviors among stakeholders. Neither of these effects is desirable. A countermeasure to eliminate the problem at the source is to establish standardized work for executives [26].

29. Thinking Lean management can work in a political workplace.*

Lean management thrives on merit and withers on wasteful politics. Highly political workplaces will not find much success in their Lean efforts. Political workplaces will lead to executive decision making that contradicts Lean management. For example, after the CEO announces the company is headed down the Lean path, the criteria for promotion are left unchanged. So people who are good at making the month, but who are lousy at understanding or applying Lean principles and practices, are the ones who get promoted. That sends the wrong message; it tells people that Lean is not so important after all. The criteria for promotion must be revised and adhered to (see Chapters 1-7 for guidance).

30. Thinking new behaviors is the key to creating Lean leaders.**

Focusing on behavior changes among the leadership team will not yield significant results because the fundamental problem rests in manager's beliefs. Beliefs drive behaviors, which, in turn, drive competencies. If you change management beliefs then you begin to create REAL Lean leaders [14, 15].

31. Mandating levels of Lean accomplishment.**

Mandating that an organization achieve pre-designated levels of Lean accomplishment by certain points in time politicizes Lean, turns Lean into a superficial game, reveals a fundamental misunderstanding of how people learn, and is inconsistent with the "Continuous Improvement" and "Respect for People" principles.

32. Leading the Lean transformation from your office.*

You have to "go see" in order to learn.

33. Not sharing profits with employees.*

Conventional management is selfish, Lean is not. Lean management requires profit sharing with employees, which will enlarge the economic pie and offer greater gains to investors. You must learn how to share the wealth. Sharing is okay; there is no rule in business that forbids sharing.

34. Making Lean complex.**

People have a tendency to make simple things complex. Lean made complex is a recipe for failure. Keep it simple. Stick to the fundamentals, and practice, practice, practice.

35. Confusing internal policies with externally mandated requirements.*

People often think that internal policies accurately reflect externally mandated requirements, when in fact they may not. Policies must be carefully examined to see if they are truly needed, and also to determine if they are consistent with Lean principles and practices. In addition, there is a tendency to keep adding policies to business as time goes by as a form of corrective action for when problems arise. However, this is normally done in the absence of root cause analysis, so there will be many policies that do not directly address the true nature of the problem. This must be corrected.

36. Confusing the financial term "value" (typically in the context of stock price) with the word "value" used in Lean management.**

In Lean management, the term "value" means the worth of a product or service (combination of price and non-price attributes) as perceived by end-use customers.

37. Thinking that leaders can opt-out of Lean.*

The top leader cannot allow anyone to opt-out of practicing Lean management, especially the other leaders.

38. Leaving out the "Respect for People" principle.*

It is not an option to leave out the "Respect for People" principle. Said another way, executives can not leave out the "Respect for People" principle and still claim to be doing Lean.

39. Thinking you know what the "Respect for People" principle means.*

It takes years of thought and practice to comprehend what the "Respect for People" principle means, and how this principle relates to the "Continuous Improvement" principle. Executives must also understand how the "Respect for People" principle relates to business strategy, goals, and metrics.

40. Thinking that Lean will one day stick.*

It is wrong for executives to think that if people practice Lean for several years, it will eventually stick; that it will become part of the company's DNA. Executives need to confront the reality that Lean does not stick. Lean requires constant attention, maintenance, and improvement to keep it alive and healthy. People keep Lean alive through the daily practice of Lean principles, processes, and tools. When the top leaders who have the interest in keeping Lean alive leave the company and are replaced with leaders who don't have the same interest, Lean dies.

41. Not planning for changes in leadership or ownership.*

Lean does not stick by itself even after 10, 25, or 50 years of effort, if new executives one day come into the company with other interests. Executives should prepare for high probability events such as changes in company ownership or changes in top leadership. Leaders need to install countermeasures to prevent outcomes that they wish to avoid. They need to do some Lean estate planning [3].

42. Keeping the same metrics and accounting system.*

The metrics and accounting system has to change and be consistent with Lean principles and practices [22, 27].

43. Cherry picking the Lean management system to obtain short-term gains.*

For over 100 years, executives have cherry-picked select concepts, methods, and tools to obtain short-term gains, guaranteeing poor results or failure.

44. Using Lean management to perpetuate a sellers' market view.*

Businesses that serve buyers' markets should be managed to that type of market, and not for sellers' markets that do not exist. This is inconsistent with the "Respect for People" principle and will undercut "Continuous Improvement" efforts.

45. Thinking that Lean management does not apply to me / us.*

Everyone says this at some time or another, due to misunderstandings, misperceptions, or inadequate explanation of Lean management. Often, it is just an excuse for not wanting to think or do anything differently. Professional people, in particular, have long viewed their work as creative and resented being treated as an element of production. Their work may or may not be creative, and the resentment is more emotional than fact based.

46. Lacking commitment to merit, logic, knowledge, detail, facts, and reality.*

A preference for organizational politics and obfuscation always derails Lean efforts.

47. Using Lean tools to fine-tune the status quo.*

Tweaking the current state in response to competitive pressures is not leadership; it is laziness, and it could be irresponsible. Seeking to fine-tune assumes that the business is already near the point of optimal tuning, which is not the case as current state value stream maps show.

48. Inability to relinquish power to subordinates.*

Lean leaders share some powers with subordinates and retain other powers that appropriately lie within the executive realm. Leaders have to relinquish power to their subordinates, just as they eventually have to do as parents with their children.

49. Isolating one's self from employees.*

Lean leaders do not stay in the office and isolate themselves from employees (or customers or other stakeholders). They engage employees in all functional areas and "go see" to understand what is really going on.

50. Hiring the wrong consultants.*

Executives typically hire consultants whose specialty is tools for short-term efficiency improvement but who represents themselves as disciples of Lean management without full knowledge of the system [28]. In other words, they are experts at "Continuous Improvement" but lack deep knowledge of the "Respect for People" principle and especially how the two principles function together.

Chapter 8 – Self-Study
Write your responses in the space provided.

 Thinking

1. Why do you think the same errors are repeated by generations of executives? Can you identify specific problems, errors, or deficiencies in undergraduate or graduate education, on-the-job-training, and executive mindset or environment that contribute to this repetition of errors? What practical countermeasures can be applied?

PROBLEM | COUNTERMEASURE

- | -
- | -
- | -
- | -
- | -
- | -
- | -
- | -
- | -

2. Can you identify any other errors that executives make in their Lean transformation?

- | -
- | -
- | -
- | -
- | -

3. Which of the 50 errors do you think have the most disastrous effect on efforts to achieve a Lean transformation?

-

-

-

-

-

Doing

1. What will you do to avoid these common errors?

Action Plan*

Who	Does What	By When

* Make sure you do not delegate that which only you should do.

2. Create a 30x40 inch visual display of these 50 errors that can be used as a reminder for executives of what not to do. Be creative; do not simply list all 50 errors.

3. Create a pocket-sized card of these 50 errors that can be used as a reminder for executives of what not to do. Be creative; do not simply list all 50 errors.

Commit These to Memory

- Each generation of managers makes the same errors.
- The ease with which errors are made underscores how dramatically different Lean management is compared to how executives normally lead and manage.
- Executives who are steeped in conventional management practice can avoid making numerous errors by being attentive to the Lean principles, "Continuous Improvement" and "Respect for People," and carefully studying and practicing Lean management every day.
- Small and large errors in executives' understanding and practice of Lean management will lead to poor results and many problems.

9

Visual Control for Lean Leaders

It is my hope that this workbook has successfully guided you through the major differences, as well as many minor differences, between conventional leadership and Lean leadership. While your cognitive understanding and perspective has been improved, learning the Lean management system and how to become a Lean leader can only take place through daily practice.

In order to get started you will need to be highly motivated. Beyond trying to inspire you, there is not much I can do to motivate you. You have to look inside yourself and at the world around you and decide whether or not you can make more meaningful contributions. I'm certain you can. The question is: will you engage in the challenge?

Another thing you will need is reminders of what to do, as this is new territory where it is easy to fall back into beliefs, behaviors, and competencies and make mistakes. This is something I can help you with.

The two-sided color page at the end of this workbook is a detachable visual control that summarizes the key points and serves as a reminder to help you practice Lean management every day [1]. I encourage you to detach this visual control and use it. It highlights the practical things you should do and how you should think about your work as an executive, spanning daily work activities to strategic work. It would be beneficial for you to laminate it in plastic to improve its long-term durability and usability.

Explanations of the words and images contained in the visual control are as follows:

Front

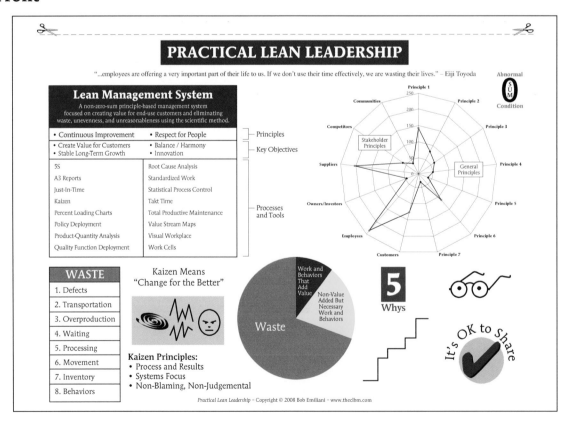

Quote by Eiji Toyoda (past Chairman and CEO of Toyota Motor Corporation)
- Reminds you that as an executive you are responsible for other people's lives, and that their lives should be used wisely.

Abnormal Condition, Zero-Sum, Caux Round Table Principles for Business Radar Chart
- Reminds you that managing a business in a zero-sum fashion leads to imbalances that create waste, unevenness, and unreasonableness. This image defines the problem you likely face and should remind you to methodically determine its many root causes and identify practical countermeasures.

Lean Management System
- Defines Lean management and reminds you that Lean is a management system that consists of two key principles, key objectives, and processes and tools used to eliminate waste, unevenness, and unreasonableness.

Waste
- Reminds you of the eight wastes.

Definition of Kaizen
- Reminds you that it means "change for the better," in a multilateral context.

Symbols for Waste, Unevenness, and Unreasonableness
- Reminds you that you have to do more than just eliminate process and behavioral waste. You must also eliminate unevenness and unreasonableness in processes and leadership behaviors.

Kaizen Principles
- Reminds you that you must use these three principles when you practice kaizen.

Pie Chart
- Reminds you that Lean management is concerned with more than just work processes. There are also leadership behaviors that add value, some that do not add value but are unavoidable, and many which are waste.

5 Whys
- Reminds you that you must do simple root cause analysis on a regular basis for the types of problems that executives face. Use the 5 Whys, fishbone diagram, or similar methods.

Eyeglasses
- Reminds you to get out of the office and go see what is happening in the workplace, and that you should periodically stand in your worker's shoes to understand what they are experiencing and make improvements.

Stair Steps
- Reminds you that continuous improvement is a step-wise process.

It OK to Share
- Reminds you that it is OK to share. The consequence of not sharing with your stakeholders leads to the imbalances shown on the radar chart. You'll need to work on changing your belief that sharing is cost that you cannot afford. The benefits of sharing outweigh the costs.

Back

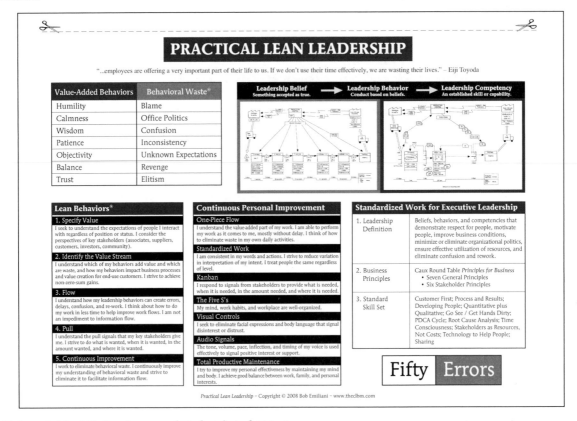

Practical Lean Leadership – Copyright © 2008 Bob Emiliani – www.theclbm.com

Value-Added Behaviors and Behavioral Waste
- Reminds you of the value-added behaviors and behavioral waste by providing a few examples.

Leadership Belief ➤ Leadership Behavior ➤ Leadership Competency
- Reminds you of how value stream maps can be used to deduce leadership beliefs, behaviors, and competencies. You should apply the process shown in Chapter 5 to deduce leadership beliefs, behaviors, and competencies for other value stream maps in your company.

Lean Behaviors
- Reminds you of what these are so you can practice them every day.

Continuous Personal Improvement
- Reminds you of what these are so you can practice them every day.

Standardized Work for Executive Leadership
- Reminds you of the leadership definition, business principles, and standard skill set so you can practice them every day.

50 Errors
- Reminds you of the 50 common errors that executives make when implementing Lean management, so you will hopefully avoid all of them.

> **Carry the visual control with you in your notebook and make a copy of each side to display in your office.**

Chapter 9 – Self-Study
Write your responses in the space provided.

 Doing

1. The visual control for Lean leaders is a reminder to do many things differently than you have done in the past. The things you need to do differently will occur daily. Look at your schedule over the last several weeks and identify 20 things that must change in your daily schedule as a result of using the visual control and other things you learned in this workbook.

OLD ACTIVITY

-
-
-
-
-
-
-
-
-
-

NEW ACTIVITY

-
-
-
-
-
-
-
-
-
-

Remember, you cannot become a Lean leader by doing the same things you have always done. Your daily schedule must change, in addition to your beliefs, behaviors, and competencies.

10

Lean Leader Performance Feedback

Chapter Highlights

- Understand performance measurement in a Lean business
- Apply rules for Lean metrics
- Implement a new Lean leadership performance metric

Your diligent daily practice of the things you learned in this workbook will make you a better leader and also result in improved financial and non-financial performance. Executives will want to be certain that their efforts are having a positive impact on the enterprise. This feedback will come from a variety of established sources including some of the financial and non-financial metrics that are currently in use.

However, upon close examination you will find that many of your long-established company metrics are inconsistent with Lean principles and practices. They reflect the view that you are serving sellers' markets, rather than buyers' markets. So you will first have to carefully scrutinize each one of your financial and non-financial metrics to ensure they are consistent with Lean principles and practices, eliminate waste, unevenness, and unreasonableness, and facilitate the flow of material, information, and value-added behaviors. This will take some time, but it is essential work that must be done.

Some metrics will be fine and can be used as-is. Some metrics will cause problems but can be easily eliminated or modified, or their importance in decision making can be greatly de-emphasized. Other metrics will cause problems but may be much harder to eliminate or modify. In these causes, a team should establish a plan to make the changes necessary to the metrics to eliminate or modify them in an orderly manner.

The general rules for Lean metrics are summarized in Table 10-1 [1, 2]:

Table 10-1

Characteristic	Explanation
Must support the strategy	Metrics that do not support the strategy will cause confusion, misunderstanding, misalignment. Expectations will become ambiguous. People will lose focus on the strategy if metrics appear to be disconnected or contradictory.
Few in number	Too many metrics cause confusion and unnecessary competition among individuals or departments. Most people can only remember a few things.
Mostly non-financial	Most people do not understand financial metrics. Instead, use metrics that people can relate to such as time, distance, number of defects, area (i.e. square footage), number of pieces, number of people, etc.
Motivate the right behaviors	The purpose of the metric is to eliminate waste. Metrics for the sake of metrics is waste. Metrics that do not support the elimination of waste are not helpful. The metrics should focus people's efforts on improvement.
Simple and easy to understand	Most people have many things on their minds. Management has a responsibility to make work easy for people to understand. Use measures that connect processes, such as time.
Measure process, not the people	Measuring people results in blame, politics, high employee turnover, etc., which is waste.
Measure actuals vs. goals	People can relate more easily to actuals and goals. Standard costs are not real numbers. Measuring variances based upon standards is time-consuming, confusing, and does not help people understand the root cause. Measuring variances against standards is misleading and is slow to respond to changes in the marketplace.
Avoid using ratios	Ratios are confusing and people have difficulty relating to them. Do not use them across the entire business. Management may use ratios in support of the type of work that management does.
Don't combine measures into a single index or create complex formulas	Indices and formulas are difficult to understand and do not help people eliminate waste. People cannot relate their work to them.
Must be timely: hourly, daily, weekly	Measures must reflect the time-scale in which work actually takes place. Monthly or quarterly measures can be out of step with the marketplace. The lag time between data collection and review often leads to poor decisions.

There is always a tendency among executives today to add new financial or non-financial metrics; for example, to create a Lean behaviors metric or a conformance to executive standardized work metric. This should not happen. Instead, scrutinize your existing metrics and eliminate those that inconsistent with Lean principles and practices and disrupt flow.

> **Your challenge is to move steadily in the direction of fewer metrics that are timely and simpler to understand and respond to.**

If you do decide to add new metrics, it should not be more than a handful. One metric that I suggest you consider links your business activities directly to your stakeholders by using the Caux Round Table *Principles for Business* [3]. Figure 10-1 shows the radar chart used in Chapter 7, question 8 of the self-study section.

Figure 10-1

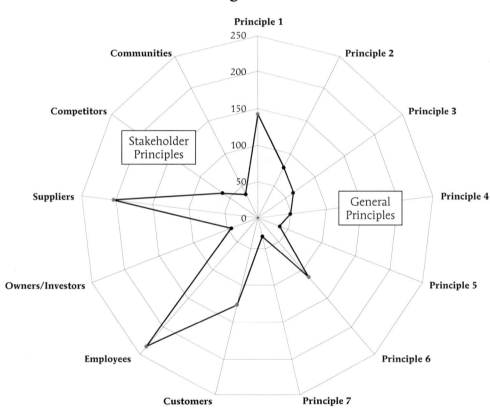

Recall that it shows people's perceptions of their organization's performance relative to the *Principles for Business*. The imbalances are significant and are the result of long-term executive commitment to zero-sum thinking and practices. There are large inconstancies for general principles 1 and 6 and the stakeholder principles for employees, customers, and suppliers, which generates large amount of waste, unevenness, and unreasonableness, and also disrupts flow.

Second, you will need to do root cause analysis and identify practical countermeasures that will restore balance to your business as shown in Figure 10-2. As you implement countermeasures, you can then seek the participation of various stakeholder groups to anonymously identify where your organization is inconsistent with *Principles for Business* just as you did in Chapter 7, (question 8 of the self-study section). This metric, along with financial and non-financial measures that are consistent with Lean, will be a true test of your leadership.

The data can easily be collected electronically via a Web site (yours or third party) two or three times per year. You could obtain data in a couple of different ways. Solicit input from each of the stakeholder groups: customers, employees, owners/investors, suppliers, competitors, and communities. Or, solicit input from a narrower group of stakeholders – customers, employees, and suppliers – who are closest to the actual business issues and problems that you face (see Figure 10-1), and who may also provide you with a reasonably accurate representation of the views of owners/investors, competitors, and communities.

It would not be advisable to ask a given stakeholder, such as suppliers, to limit their feedback to their own stakeholder category. You should challenge them to give you a broader perspective. After all, they interact with your employees every day and surely have information about their attitudes and morale. Likewise, your suppliers probably do business with your competitors, and they are part of the community in which you operate. Some may even be investors in your business. Your suppliers – and customers and employees – know a lot more than you think.

Figure 10-2

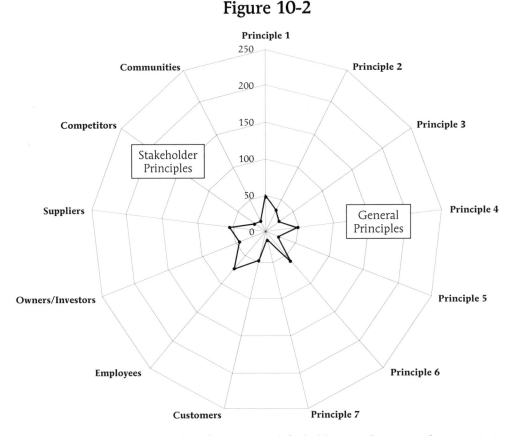

Finally, please do not become overly reliant on or deluded by numbers. Just because it is not contained in a spreadsheet does not mean it doesn't exist. Lean leaders "go see" when a problem arises and talk to people in a non-blaming, non-judgmental way to ascertain the facts. They get out of the office and constantly develop their observation skills so they can see realities and avoid being misled by the numbers.

Chapter 10 – Self-Study
Write your responses in the space provided.

 Thinking

Answer questions 3 through 9, below, then review self-study questions 3 through 9 that you answered in the Introduction. How has your perception and understanding of Lean management and strategic leadership changed?

3. What does "Continuous Improvement" mean to you? How do you define it?

4. What does "Respect for People" mean to you? How do you define it?

5. Why do you think Toyota represents the "Respect for People" principle as a larger circle compared to the "Continuous Improvement" principle?

6. Has your company been practicing Fake Lean or REAL Lean? If the answer is Fake Lean, then what do you think caused the incorrect practice of Lean management?

7. Identify five reasons why you think the "Respect for People" principle is so important in the practice of Lean management.

-

-

-

-

-

8. If someone says to you "Lean is a theory," what would you say to them to convincingly refute that perception?

9. Describe ways in which laying people off as a result of productivity improvements would be inconsistent with the "Respect for People" principle.

A major problem that has plagued Lean management for decades, as well as its antecedent Scientific Management since the early 1900s, is persistent misunderstandings, misinterpretations, and misapplications of its principles and practices, in whole or part, by executives.

Readers should seek to avoid this problem and the multitude of errors that stem from it. This can be achieved by periodically reviewing this workbook, by gaining additional knowledge of Lean management from authoritative sources, as well as daily study and practice. There are no shortcuts [4].

> **Now is a good time to go back and review Chapters 1, 2, and 3, including the Self-Study questions and the answers that you wrote.**
>
> **Schedule a time next week to review Chapters 4-10 to reinforce the learnings and avoid misunderstandings, misinterpretations, and misapplications of the Lean management system. Also review the Self-Study questions and answers in these chapters.**
>
> **Periodically review the entire workbook.**

Afterword

It has been a 13-year effort to understand the intricacies of Lean leadership and develop ways to present it that are fully consistent with Lean principles and practices, and brought to you in a more condensed and digestible form. It is my sincere hope that I have been successful in helping you see the practicality and usefulness of what is contained in this workbook.

This work clearly illuminates the intimate links between Lean management and Lean leadership. The "basic way of thinking," a new definition of leadership, Lean behaviors, continuous personal improvement, value stream mapping, kaizen, and standardized work for executives puts leadership and the challenge of leadership development in a fresh new perspective.

In addition, this approach will be much less expensive to implement. By shifting to this new approach, you will no longer need to spend so much money on traditional leadership training and leadership development programs. For example, those leadership training and development programs that present leadership fully as art; that are non-specific in terms of what to do; that do not show the connections between beliefs, behaviors, and competencies; and, those that do not explicitly present specific links to daily workplace activities. The savings should be invested in kaizen and shared with your employees.

Efforts to get executives to adopt a different system of management have always been a big challenge. So I have many concerns. The first one is that executives will succumb to erroneous views such as: "this is theory," "we're different," "we're already doing that," etc. Convincing yourself that you know what you do not know is self-defeating, and you will eventually drive your company into difficulties that could have been avoided.

A second concern is that executives will maintain their bad habits and selectively adopt what is presented in this workbook; in other words, cherry pick some ideas and methods that suit short-term interests and cast others aside. Executives have a long history of doing this [1-3] despite the fact that it does not serve anyone's interests and usually leads to failure.

A third concern is that executives will sabotage their own interests by promoting unqualified people to lead Lean efforts. It should be obvious that the political approach to hiring and promotion is not favored by Lean leaders. They adhere to a merit-based approach. This will be a difficult transition for most leaders unless value stream maps and standardized work for executives become part of the performance appraisal, incentive compensation, and promotion processes.

A fourth concern is that executives who were raised in conventional management will not find the motivation and desire to study, learn, and practice Lean management. In the short-term, what is in it for them? Probably nothing, but executives do have big egos and are concerned about their legacies, the future of the company, etc. The motivation could develop from these long-term interests that actually do exist.

I also have some concerns for those executives who do find the motivation and desire to study, learn, and practice Lean management. Will they have the personal discipline to maintain a steady course, even through bad business times? Will they be discriminating and avoid sources of information and help that promote Lean as tools or in other narrow ways? Will they get confused or be influenced by the abundance of low quality information on the topic of Lean management? Will they walk the talk, or just talk and then go play golf? Will they lead by example, or will they delegate that which only they can do (see Appendix III)? Do they recognize the level of effort they must put in to enforcing the daily use of Lean principles and practices throughout the organization?

Executives will be tempted to focus their attention on continuous improvement processes and tools because they appear to offer the biggest near-term opportunity to lower costs and obtain higher profits. But these appearances will deceive you, and you could become the newest new member of an ignominious club. If all you do is support the use of continuous improvement tools, then you will fail just as legions of executives who have failed before you over the last 100 years [3]. When that happens, please do a root cause analysis of why you failed. You will find out that a principal root cause was that you ignored people, your key stakeholders, and that the practical countermeasure to avoid recurrence of this error is "Respect for People."

It is important for executives to recognize that the Toyota you see today is not the Toyota of 1937 when it began its automobile business, with regards to "Continuous Improvement" and "Respect for People." They have steadily evolved and improved upon their practice of both principles over time. They did not practice "Respect for People" well at first, but Toyota executives kept thinking and learning what this principle means. Toyota still has many more opportunities to continuously improve its understanding and practice of the "Respect for People" principle, which should not be a surprise because it is the more challenging of the two principles to comprehend and practice.

Likewise, your understanding and practice of the "Respect for People" principle will be poor at first, particularly if your workplace resembles the current state value stream map shown in Figure 5-2a. But it will get better as you understand what this principle means and how to make it work. You too will have the challenge of continuously improving your understanding and practice of the "Respect for People" principle. This workbook should be a very helpful start.

One of your first big challenges will be to figure how to equitably share the gains your company achieves in productivity improvement, cost reduction, and improved profitability with employees (higher wages), customers (lower prices), suppliers (fair prices), and investors (dividends).

Your second big challenge will be to recognize that profit sharing is consistent with the "Respect for People" principle, and that it does not have to come at the expense of investors' interests. Do not assume there is no return on investment from profit sharing. A quarterly profit sharing plan using the formula of 15 percent pre-tax income divided by straight time wages for hourly and salaried employees, with a uniform profit sharing goal of 20 percent straight time wages is appropriate [4]. You may also need to re-think your executive pay and bonus plans to make sure it too is consistent with the "Respect for People" principle with regard to employees and investors.

You have to be totally consistent. If not, you will learn first-hand how authoritarian or exploitative use of Lean management, while seemingly expedient, will severely undermine your efforts. Penny-wise, pound-foolish decisions are a hallmark of conventional management [5] that must be overcome.

This workbook has given you specific and actionable frameworks for Lean leadership development. There is much you can do on your own and as a management team to practice what you have learned in this workbook, including using the visual control. It should keep you very busy for some time, provided you are motivated to improve and develop the discipline to practice every day.

Afterword

Some readers will want to go a step further and integrate what they have learned in this workbook with their company's overall strategy and top-level planning processes. For the latter you can turn to policy deployment (Hoshin Kanri) [6-9]. It is a process that engages senior leaders in aligning their organizations' customer-focused strategic objectives and goals with daily activities consistent with available resources.

Policy deployment is a very effective process for focusing organizations on what matters most and avoiding distractions that do not support the company's purpose. It can help ensure that an executive team practices Lean leadership as presented in this workbook every day, and assists with providing valuable feedback on the leadership team's performance.

If, over time, you can do what is presented in this workbook in a consistent and disciplined manner, and also extend this through future generations of managers, then your organization will enjoy many benefits including long-term Toyota-like competitive advantage.

In closing, it is impossible for anyone to know it all when it comes to Lean management. In the words of Katsuaki Watanabe, President of Toyota Motor Corporation [10]:

> **"There's no end to the process of learning about the Toyota Way.
> I don't think I have a complete understanding even today,
> and I have worked for the company for 43 years."**

Endnotes

Preface

[1] The phrase "Lean management system" is used throughout this book. A synonymous phrase is "Lean business system," which, like the previous phrase, indicates broad application of Lean principles and practices throughout an enterprise. While synonymous, the phrase "Lean business system" is not used because some readers may come from other types of organizations such as government, non-profit, or education, where the word "business" may not resonate with them. In addition, the phrase "management system" has historical significance dating back to the early 1900s Scientific Management era, when efforts were first made by Frederick W. Taylor to distinguish stand-alone productivity and efficiency improvement tools from a larger system of organized management principles and practices. Other phrases such as "Lean operating system" and "Lean production system" are not used because they indicate a narrow application of Lean that is largely restricted to manufacturing or service operations activities. This meaning, while commonly used since the late 1970s, has contributed to widespread misunderstandings, misapplication, and narrow application of Lean management.

[2] "Management Tools and Trends 2007," D. Rigby and B. Bilodeau, Bain & Company, March 2007

[3] The author's tone is serious because business is serious; people's lives depend upon the thinking and decision making capabilities of their leaders. This book challenges leaders to improve in a very direct fashion, much the same way that a golf coach or music teacher challenges their most promising students to improve. They push hard – but for good reasons.

Introduction

[1] Some excellent books were available to English-speaking readers in the 1980s to help guide Lean transformations including: S. Shingo, *Study of 'Toyota' Production System from Industrial Engineering Viewpoint*, Japan Management Association, distributed by Productivity Inc., Cambridge, MA, 1981; Y. Monden, *Toyota Production System: Practical Approach to Production Management*, Industrial Engineering and Management Press, Norcross, GA, 1983; T. Ohno, *Toyota Production System*, Productivity Press, Portland, OR, 1988; T. Ohno, *Workplace Management*, Productivity Press, Cambridge, MA, 1988. Notable books from the 1990s include: J. Womack, D. Jones, and D. Roos, *The Machine that Changed the World*, Rawson Associates, New York, NY, 1990; Y. Monden, *Toyota Management System: Linking the Seven Key Functional Areas*, Productivity Press, Portland, OR, 1993; J. Womack and D. Jones, *Lean Thinking*, Simon & Schuster, New York, NY, 1996; T. Fujimoto, *The Evolution of a Manufacturing System at Toyota*, Oxford University Press, New York, NY, 1999.

[2] See J. McMillan, *Games Strategies and Managers*, Oxford University Press, 1992, p. 26. The total gains are constant in zero-sum transactions, which means that winners gain at the expense of losers. Also note that business ethics training will be largely useless in companies where top management's dominant view of business is zero-sum. Non-zero-sum means all parties share in the gains (or losses).

[3] W. Tsutsui, *Manufacturing Ideology: Scientific Management in Twentieth-Century Japan*, Princeton University Press, Princeton New Jersey, 1998

[4] M.L. Emiliani, "Lean Behaviors," *Management Decision*, Vol. 36, No. 9, pp. 615-631, 1998

[5] M.L. Emiliani, "Continuous Personal Improvement," *Journal of Workplace Learning*, Vol. 10, No. 1, pp. 29-38, 1998

[6] M.L. Emiliani, "Linking Leaders' Beliefs to Their Behaviors and Competencies," *Management Decision*, Vol. 41, No. 9, pp. 893-910, 2003

Endnotes

[7] M.L. Emiliani and D.J. Stec, "Using Value Stream Maps to Improve Leadership," *Leadership and Organizational Development Journal*, Vol. 25, No. 8, pp. 622-645, 2004

[8] M.L. Emiliani, "Standardized Work for Executive Leadership," *Leadership and Organizational Development Journal*, Vol. 29, No. 1, pp. 24-46, 2008

[9] B. Emiliani, with D. Stec, L. Grasso, and J. Stodder, *Better Thinking, Better Results: Case Study and Analysis of an Enterprise-Wide Lean Transformation*, second edition, The CLBM, LLC, Wethersfield, Conn., 2007

[10] "The Toyota Way 2001," Toyota Motor Corporation, internal document, Toyota City, Japan, April 2001

1 What is Lean Management?

[1] J. Womack, D. Jones, and D. Roos, *The Machine that Changed the World*, Rawson Associates, New York, NY, 1990, p. 13

[2] "The Toyota Way 2001," Toyota Motor Corporation, internal document, Toyota City, Japan, April 2001

[3] J. Liker, *The Toyota Way*, McGraw-Hill, New York, NY, 2004

[4] This is Emiliani's definition of Lean management. It was developed after years of study and practice of Lean management, including research into the antecedent of Lean, Scientific Management, dating to the late 1800s. The reason why this definition is used is because Lean management has not been previously defined by others or in books such as *Lean Thinking* or in the *Lean Lexicon* glossary (see Note [5]). This is a significant omission, brought about in part by persistent narrow characterization of Lean as a manufacturing or production system, which has resulted in a proliferation of poor or erroneous definitions and associated misunderstandings.

[5] *Lean Lexicon*, third edition, version 3.0, Lean Enterprise Institute, Cambridge, MA, September 2006

[6] T. Ohno, *Toyota Production System*, Productivity Press, Portland, OR, 1988, p. 58

[7] Ibid, pp. 19-20. Note that the waste of processing is commonly misunderstood as overprocessing. The waste is processing itself, not overprocessing, because it challenges people to ask if the entire process can be eliminated rather than just a part of the process.

2 How Lean Leaders Think

[1] "The Toyota Way 2001," Toyota Motor Corporation, internal document, Toyota City, Japan, April 2001

[2] J. Liker, *The Toyota Way*, McGraw-Hill, New York, NY, 2004

[3] S. Hino, *Inside the Mind of Toyota*, Productivity Press, New York, NY, 2006

[4] S. Basu, *Corporate Purpose: Why it Matters More than Strategy*, Garland Publishing, New York, NY, 1999

[5] Toyota's corporate purpose and business principles can be found at http://www.toyota.co.jp/en/vision/message/index.html, as well as http://www.toyota.co.jp/en/vision/philosophy/index.html and http://www.toyota.co.jp/en/vision/sustainability/index.html

[6] B. Emiliani, with D. Stec, L. Grasso, and J. Stodder, *Better Thinking, Better Results: Case Study and Analysis of an Enterprise-Wide Lean Transformation*, second edition, The CLBM, LLC, Wethersfield, Conn., 2007

[7] B. Emiliani, *REAL LEAN: Understanding the Lean Management System*, Volume One, The CLBM, LLC, Wethersfield, Conn., 2007

[8] B. Emiliani, *REAL LEAN: Critical Issues and Opportunities in Lean Management*, Volume Two, The CLBM, LLC, Wethersfield, Conn., 2007

Practical Lean Leadership

3 A Better Definition of Leadership

[1] J. Maxwell, *21 Irrefutable Laws of Leadership*, Thomas Nelson, Inc., Nashville, TN, 1998

[2] F. Hesselbein, M. Goldsmith, and R. Beckhard, editors, *The Leader of the Future*, Foreword by Peter Drucker, Jossey-Bass, New York NY, 1996, p. ii

[3] W. Bennis, *Leaders: Strategies for Taking Charge*, HarperCollins Publishers, New York, NY, 2003, p. 78

[4] M.L. Emiliani, "Standardized Work for Executive Leadership," *Leadership and Organizational Development Journal*, Vol. 29, No. 1, pp. 24-46, 2008. Emiliani created and has been using the improved definition of leadership in executive training since 2003.

4 Lean Leadership Behaviors

[1] M.L. Emiliani, "Lean Behaviors," *Management Decision*, Vol. 36, No. 9, pp. 615-631, 1998. Emiliani coined the term "Lean Behaviors" in August 1996 and "Behavioral Waste" in 1998.

[2] M.L. Emiliani, unpublished research, 2001-2007.

[3] J. Womack and D. Jones, *Lean Thinking*, Simon & Schuster, New York, NY, 1996

[4] M.L. Emiliani, "Continuous Personal Improvement," *Journal of Workplace Learning*, Vol. 10, No. 1, pp. 29-38, 1998

[5] Adapted from *Lean Lexicon*, third edition, version 3.0, Lean Enterprise Institute, Cambridge, MA, September 2006

[6] After World War II (circa 1949), the U.S. Occupation authorities introduced Japanese managers to the "Training Within Industry" (TWI) program. One facet of that training was "Job Relations," which was intended to teach front-line supervisors how to improve their relationships with workers. Many of these supervisors would later become top company executives. This helped form the basis for the non-zero-sum leadership behaviors that are commonly found in Lean businesses. TWI's foundation for good supervisor-worker relations included visual controls (cards) that said: 1. Let each worker know how he is getting along; 2. Give credit when due; 3) Tell people in advance about changes that will affect them; 4) Make the best use of each person's ability. TWI's specific steps for handling supervisor-worker relationship problems visual controls (cards) that said: 1. Get the facts; 2. Weigh and decide; 3. Take action; 4. Check results. See J. Huntzinger, "The Roots of Lean: The Origin of Japanese Management and Kaizen," http://www.superfactory.com/articles/Huntzinger_roots_lean.pdf, June 2005. See also A. Smalley, "TWI Influence on TPS and Kaizen," http://www.superfactory.com/articles/Smalley_Kato_TWI.htm, May 2006

[7] Simple and well-constructed employee surveys can provide useful information regarding the practice of Lean behaviors among top managers and supervision. See B. Emiliani, with D. Stec, L. Grasso, and J. Stodder, *Better Thinking, Better Results: Case Study and Analysis of an Enterprise-Wide Lean Transformation*, second edition, The CLBM, LLC, Wethersfield, Conn., 2007, pp. 118-120 and p. 135, note 13.

5 Value Stream Maps as a Leadership Development Tool

[1] J. Womack and D. Jones, *Lean Thinking*, Simon & Schuster, New York, NY, 1996

[2] M. Rother and J. Shook, *Learning to See*, Lean Enterprise Institute, Boston, MA, 1999

[3] D. Tapping and T. Shuker, *Value Stream Management for the Lean Office*, Productivity Press, New York, NY, 2003

[4] B. Maskell, "Costing the Value Stream," Lean Enterprise Institute Value Stream Management Summit, Orlando, FL, March 19, 2001

[5] D. Simons and R. Mason, "Lean *and* Green: Doing More with Less," *ECR Journal*, Vol. 3, No. 1, Spring, 2003, pp. 84-91

[6] A. Lucia and R. Lepsinger, *The Art and Science of Competency Models*, Jossey-Bass/Pfeiffer, San

Francisco, CA, 1999

[7] M.L. Emiliani and D.J. Stec, "Using Value Stream Maps to Improve Leadership," *Leadership and Organizational Development Journal*, Vol. 25, No. 8, pp. 622-645, 2004

[8] M.L. Emiliani, "Linking Leaders' Beliefs to Their Behaviors and Competencies," *Management Decision*, Vol. 41, No. 9, pp. 893-910, 2003

6 What Executives Need to Know About Kaizen

[1] M. Imai, *Kaizen: The Key to Japan's Competitive Success*, McGraw-Hill, New York, NY, 1986

[2] M. Imai, *Gemba Kaizen*, McGraw-Hill, New York, NY, 1997

[3] M.L. Emiliani, "Origins of Lean Management in America: The Role of Connecticut Businesses," *Journal of Management History*, Vol. 12, No. 2, pp. 167-184, 2006, http://www.theclbm.com/articles/lean_in_conn.pdf

[4] B. Emiliani, with D. Stec, L. Grasso, and J. Stodder, *Better Thinking, Better Results: Case Study and Analysis of an Enterprise-Wide Lean Transformation*, second edition, The CLBM, LLC, Wethersfield, Conn., 2007, Chapters 3 and 4

[5] M. Imai, "Basics of Kaizen I," Kaizen Institute of America seminar at The Hartford Graduate Center, Hartford, Conn., March 1990, p. II-3

7 Standardized Work for Executive Leadership

[1] For an excellent example of standard work for plant-level managers and supervisors, see D. Mann, *Creating a Lean Culture: Tools to Sustain Lean Conversions*, Productivity Press, New York, NY, 2005

[2] M. Imai, Y. Iwata, C. Nakao, and A. Takenaka, "The Text for JIT/Toyota Production System Seminar," Kaizen Institute of America seminar at The Hartford Graduate Center, Hartford, Conn., May 2-3, 1988

[3] "How to Implement Kaizen in Manufacturing," Shingijutsu Co., Ltd, Gifu, Japan, 1992

[4] J. Liker and D. Meier, *The Toyota Way Fieldbook*, McGraw-Hill, New York, NY, 2006, Chapter 6

[5] *Standardized work* is not the same as *work standards*. Work standards are imposed on workers by managers as part of a financial effort to create standard unit costs used in absorption accounting systems. Standardized work is the creation of the best known method of work at a given point in time that yields the highest quality, least amount of waste, and lowest total cost. Work standards focus on the worker, are thought by managers to be the one best way the work can be performed, and are used as a carrot or stick against employees. In contrast, standardized work focuses on the process and is used to establish a baseline for continuous improvement in which workers and managers participate. See note [3].

[6] C. Going, *Principles of Industrial Engineering*, McGraw-Hill, New York, NY, 1911, pp. 26-31

[7] D. Kimball, *Principles of Industrial Organization*, McGraw-Hill, New York, NY, 1913, p. 245

[8] *Lean Lexicon*, third edition, version 3.0, Lean Enterprise Institute, Cambridge, MA, 2006, p. 85

[9] M.L. Emiliani, "Standardized Work for Executive Leadership," *Leadership and Organizational Development Journal*, Vol. 29, No. 1, pp. 24-46, 2008

[10] See J. McMillan, *Games Strategies and Managers*, Oxford University Press, 1992, p. 26. The total gains are constant in zero-sum transactions, which means that winners gain at the expense of losers. Few executives bother to consider if the "quick hits" they seek result in "quick losses" elsewhere in the organizations or among their key stakeholders. They need to understand this.

8 Fifty Errors to Avoid

[1] F.W. Taylor, *The Principles of Scientific Management*, Harper & Brothers Publishers, New York, NY, 1911. Also see "Testimony Before the House Committee" in *Scientific Management: Comprising Shop Management, Principles of Scientific Management, Testimony Before the House*

Committee, F.W. Taylor, with foreword by Harlow S. Person, Harper & Brothers Publishers, New York, NY, 1947.

[2] W. Tsutsui, *Manufacturing Ideology: Scientific Management in Twentieth-Century Japan*, Princeton University Press, Princeton New Jersey, 1998

[3] B. Emiliani, *REAL LEAN: Critical Issues and Opportunities in Lean Management*, Volume Two, The CLBM, LLC, Wethersfield, Conn., 2007

[4] "Many good companies try to practice kaizen and use various TPS tools. But what is important is having all the elements together as a system. It must be practiced every day in a consistent manner – not in spurts – in a concrete way...," F. Cho, Chairman of Toyota Motor Corporation.

[5] M. Imai, "Basics of Kaizen I," Kaizen Institute of America seminar at The Hartford Graduate Center, Hartford, Conn., March 1990, p. II-3

[6] J. Liker and D. Meier, *The Toyota Way Fieldbook*, McGraw-Hill, New York, NY, 2006, Chapter 6.

[7] Y. Monden, *Target Costing and Kaizen Costing*, Productivity Press, Portland, OR, 1995

[8] T. Ohno, *Toyota Production System*, Productivity Press, Portland, OR, 1988

[9] M.L. Emiliani, "Lean Behaviors," *Management Decision*, Vol. 36, No. 9, pp. 615-631, 1998

[10] LeanBlog Podcast #21 - Norman Bodek, "Building People,"
http://kanban.blogspot.com/2007/03/leanblog-podcast-21-norman-bodek.html

[11] "The Toyota Way 2001," Toyota Motor Corporation, internal document, Toyota City, Japan, April 2001

[12] J. Womack and D. Jones, *Lean Thinking*, Simon & Schuster, New York, NY, 1996

[13] B. Emiliani, *REAL LEAN: Understanding the Lean Management System*, Volume One, The CLBM, LLC, Wethersfield, Conn., 2007

[14] M.L. Emiliani, "Linking Leaders' Beliefs to Their Behaviors and Competencies," *Management Decision*, Vol. 41, No. 9, pp. 893-910, 2003

[15] M.L. Emiliani and D.J. Stec, "Using Value Stream Maps to Improve Leadership," *Leadership and Organizational Development Journal*, Vol. 25, No. 8, pp. 622-645, 2004

[16] These practical books can help guide your Lean transformation: T. Ohno, *Toyota Production System*, Productivity Press, Portland, OR, 1988; Y. Monden, *Toyota Production System: An Integrated Approach to Just-In-Time*, third edition, Industrial Engineering and Management Press, Norcross, GA, 1998; Y. Monden, *Toyota Management System: Linking the Seven Key Functional Areas*, Productivity Press, Portland, OR, 1993; T. Fujimoto, *The Evolution of a Manufacturing System at Toyota*, Oxford University Press, New York, NY, 1999; J. Liker, *The Toyota Way*, McGraw-Hill, New York, NY, 2004; S. Hino, *Inside the Mind of Toyota*, Productivity Press, New York, NY, 2006; *Better Thinking, Better Results: Case Study and Analysis of an Enterprise-Wide Lean Transformation*, B. Emiliani, with D. Stec, L. Grasso, and J. Stodder, second edition, The CLBM, LLC, Wethersfield, Conn., 2007

[17] Think of a book that teaches medical students the correct way to do a surgical procedure. The book is not theory. A physician who ignores the practical things taught in the book and instead chooses to do the work in a completely different manner is working under a new set of assumptions – a new theory – that will likely cause harm to the patient. In a similar way, executives who ignore the practical advice in a book because they mistakenly see it as theory will cause harm to the enterprise and its stakeholders.

[18] G. Hamel and C. Prahalad, "The Core Competence of the Corporation," *Harvard Business Review*, Vol. 68, No. 3, May-June, 1990, pp. 79-93.

[19] S. Basu, *Corporate Purpose: Why it Matters More than Strategy*, Garland Publishing, New York, NY, 1999. Also see http://www.toyota.co.jp/en/vision/message/index.html, as well as
http://www.toyota.co.jp/en/vision/philosophy/index.html and
http://www.toyota.co.jp/en/vision/sustainability/index.html

[20] Do not assume that the metrics contained in your expensive enterprise software system are consistent with Lean. In many cases they are inconsistent and will drive people to do things that conflict with Lean management, which will slow down and confuse your Lean transformation efforts. To gain a better understanding of metrics that are consistent with Lean management, see *Better Thinking, Better Results: Case Study and Analysis of an Enterprise-Wide Lean Transformation*, B. Emiliani, with D. Stec, L. Grasso, and J. Stodder, second edition, The CLBM, LLC, Wethersfield, Conn., 2007, *Practical Lean Accounting*, B. Maskell and B. Baggaley, Productivity Press, New York, NY, 2004, and *Real Numbers: Management Accounting in a Lean Organization*, J. Cunningham and O. Fiume, Managing Times Press, Durham, NC, 2003

[21] M.L. Emiliani, "Executive Decision Making Traps and B2B Online Reverse Auctions," *Supply Chain Management: An International Journal*, Vol. 11, No. 1, 2006, pp. 6-9

[22] M.L. Emiliani, D.J. Stec, and L.P. Grasso, "Unintended Responses to a Traditional Purchasing Performance Metric," *Supply Chain Management: An International Journal*, Vol. 10, No. 3, 2005, pp. 150-156

[23] J. Dyer and K. Nobeoka, "Creating and Managing a High-Performance Knowledge Sharing Network: The Toyota Case," *Strategic Management Journal*, Vol. 21, 2000, pp. 345-367

[24] *Better Thinking, Better Results: Case Study and Analysis of an Enterprise-Wide Lean Transformation*, B. Emiliani, with D. Stec, L. Grasso, and J. Stodder, second edition, The CLBM, LLC, Wethersfield, Conn., 2007

[25] Think of an industrial robot. Its movement is computer numerically controlled. Robots are dumb compared to human intelligence. Why make a business dumb by focusing so strongly on computer numerical control (i.e. financial software systems and financial metrics)? You reduce the intelligence of your business from human to machine. That is anti-Lean. CEOs unwittingly program people to perform limited functions and to narrowly constrain decision making which result in an inability to adapt to changing circumstances.

[26] M.L. Emiliani, "Standardized Work for Executive Leadership," *Leadership and Organizational Development Journal*, Vol. 29, No. 1, pp. 24-46, 2008

[27] B. Maskell and B. Baggaley, *Practical Lean Accounting*, Productivity Press, New York, NY, 2004, and J. Cunningham and O. Fiume, *Real Numbers: Management Accounting in a Lean Organization*, Managing Times Press, Durham, NC, 2003

[28] See Harlow S. Person in *Scientific Management in American Industry*, Harlow S. Person, editor, The Taylor Society, Harper and Brothers Publishers, New York, NY, 1929, chapter 1, pp. 12-13 and D. Nelson, "Industrial Engineering and the Industrial Enterprise, 1890-1940," pp. 38-43, in *Coordination and Information: Historical Perspectives on the Organization of Enterprise*, N. Lamoreaux and D. Raff, editors, The University of Chicago Press, Chicago, Il., 1995

9 Visual Control for Lean Leaders

[1] The origins of this type of visual control date back to my undergraduate and graduate school days in the between 1976 and 1988. I was always puzzled how at the end of each course the professors never summarized the most important points that we students absolutely must remember because we will likely find them to be very useful in real life some years later. Instead, students simply take the final exam and walk out of the classroom. This leaves it up to individual students to decide what is or is not important or worth remembering from the course. This is no good. It turns out that much of what we learn seems to us as not having been very important, which is why as adults we often say: "I don't use 90% of what I learned in college." The professors work hard, students work hard, and therefore the outcome of a course should be more concrete in terms of key learnings. So soon after I left industry to join academia, I started to teach leadership to executives in training courses. In that context, I quickly became very explicit about the key takeaways that what I wanted executives to have and created visual controls much like the one contained in this workbook.

The visual controls were always well-received by executives, so I decided to introduce them into the university setting where I teach mainly adult working professional seeking graduate degrees. The visual control first migrated into a graduate course I teach on innovative leadership, and later was introduced into other undergraduate and graduate courses in supply chain management and management failure analysis. Students consistently express positive feedback about the visual control and the enjoy the detailed explanation I give in the last class of the semester explaining what I think they must remember from the course and apply at work.

10 Lean Leader Performance Feedback

[1] B. Emiliani, with D. Stec, L. Grasso, and J. Stodder, *Better Thinking, Better Results: Case Study and Analysis of an Enterprise-Wide Lean Transformation*, second edition, The CLBM, LLC, Wethersfield, Conn., 2007

[2] J. Cunningham and O. Fiume, *Real Numbers: Management Accounting in a Lean Organization*, Managing Times Press, Durham, NC, 2003

[3] Caux Round Table *Principles for Business*, http://www.cauxroundtable.org/principles.html

[4] Because there are no shortcuts, many executives will read this book and say or think: "It's too hard." If you find yourself saying this, then perhaps you are not in the right job; maybe you can better serve the company in a different position. There is no shame in recognizing this. In the words of Henry Gantt, a noted engineer and prominent practitioner of 1900s era Scientific Management: "Among the obstacles to the introduction of this system is the fact that it forces everybody to do his duty. Many a man in authority wants a system that will force everybody else to do his duty, but will allow him to do as he pleases... He must either learn to perform his duty or yield his place..." *Work, Wages, and Profits*, second edition, H.L. Gantt, The Engineering Magazine Company, New York, NY, 1919, pp. 162-163.

Afterword

[1] Harlow S. Person in *Scientific Management in American Industry*, The Taylor Society, Harper and Brothers Publishers, New York, NY, 1929

[2] W. Tsutsui, *Manufacturing Ideology: Scientific Management in Twentieth-Century Japan*, Princeton University press, Princeton New Jersey, 1998

[3] B. Emiliani, *REAL LEAN: Critical Issues and Opportunities in Lean Management*, Volume Two, The CLBM, LLC, Wethersfield, Conn., 2007

[4] B. Emiliani, with D. Stec, L. Grasso, and J. Stodder, *Better Thinking, Better Results: Case Study and Analysis of an Enterprise-Wide Lean Transformation*, second edition, The CLBM, LLC, Wethersfield, Conn., 2007

[5] A common example is that in the drive to cut costs, the only thing that matters to senior management is to pay cheaper prices for purchased goods and services. It does not have to make any sense, other than the price is lower. In Lean management, the decision has to make sense, which sometimes means the purchase price cannot be reduced, or may even have to increase.

[6] Y. Akao, editor, *Hoshin Kanri*, Productivity Press, Inc., Portland, OR, 1991

[7] M. Cowley and E. Domb, *Beyond Strategic Vision: Effective Corporate Action with Hoshin Planning*, Butterworth-Heinemann, New York, NY, 1997

[8] P. Dennis, *Getting the Right Things Done: A Leader's Guide to Planning and Execution*, Lean Enterprise Institute, Cambridge, MA, 2006

[9] A common error that consultants and executives make is to structure their policy deployment (also called "strategy deployment") to have a narrow and selfish focus on improving the company's financial performance. Favorable financial performance is the reward for doing good work, not the objective. Policy deployment is the process used to ensure that the right work is done and that good work is done. If correctly linked to corporate purpose and strategy and properly execut-

ed, favorable financial results will follow. The correct way to set up policy deployment is to make sure it is balanced among the interests of all stakeholders – customers, employees, suppliers, investors, and the community – not solely investors. If this is not done, then policy deployment simply becomes another tool used by executives to perpetuate their long-standing zero-sum business practices. This was never the intent of policy deployment and should be avoided. Further, using policy deployment to advance zero-sum practices is inconsistent with the "Respect for People" principle and can inadvertently undercut continuous improvement efforts.

[10] Reprinted by permission of *Harvard Business Review*. From "Lessons from Toyota's Long Drive," *Harvard Business Review*, by Thomas A. Stewart and Anand P. Raman, July-August 2007, p. 80. Copyright © 2007 by the Harvard Business School Publishing Corporation; all rights reserved.

Appendix I
[1] J. Liker, *The Toyota Way*, McGraw-Hill, New York, NY, 2004, Chapters 18-20
[2] J. Liker and D. Meier, *The Toyota Way Fieldbook*, McGraw-Hill, New York, NY, 2006, Chapter 8, 13-18

Appendix II
[1] See http://www.cauxroundtable.org/principles.html

Appendix III
[1] M.L. Emiliani and D.J. Stec, "Leaders Lost in Transformation," *Leadership and Organizational Development Journal*, Vol. 26, No. 5, pp. 370-387, 2005

Appendix I – Example of 5 Whys Root Cause Analysis Method

The "5 Whys" is a simple method of root cause analysis that all executives should use in addition to fishbone diagrams. It is a structured investigation of cause-and-effect using Socratic questioning. The 5 Whys method is normally done in a small group setting, but can and should be done on an individual basis, and also done daily to gain proficiency. Common errors in doing the 5 Whys include:

- The answer is not related to the question
- Mixing multiple lines of thought
- Stop at the fifth why
- Countermeasure is not practical or implementable

Below is an example of a 5 Whys analysis that exams why managers generally insist on adhering to plans developed months ago which are no longer realistic.

Problem: Senior managers adhere to plans that are no longer realistic.

Question	Answer	Countermeasure*
1. Why do most senior managers try to adhere to plans?	Plans are linked to performance and compensation.	• Improve planning process to eliminate rigidity in planning. • Link performance and compensation to overall company goals.
2. Why are plans linked to performance and compensation?	To drive people to meet company objectives.	• Use kaizen to improve processes instead of driving people.
3. Why drive people to meet company objectives?	To meet commitments to _____.	• Establish process to avoid over-committing.
4. Why is it important to meet commitments to _____?	To satisfy _____.	•
5. Why is it important to satisfy _____?	To keep them happy.	•
6. Why keep them happy?	To avoid problems.	• Use same processes for identifying and correcting problems for all levels of employees [1, 2].
7. Why do they want to avoid problems?	To avoid getting blamed, job loss, demotion, pay cut, etc.	• Establish no-blame environment.
8. Why do people want to avoid blame, job loss, demotion, pay cut, etc?	It's embarrassing, look bad in front of others, stressful, loss of self-esteem.	• Focus on the process, not the people.

* In Lean management, countermeasures are not thought of as solutions because it is virtually impossible for people to completely understand a problem at any given point in time. Instead, countermeasures are practical actions based upon current knowledge of the problem that should prevent recurrence.

Appendix II – Caux Round Table *Principles for Business* (1994)
Reprinted with permission of the Caux Round Table [1]

Introduction

The Caux Round Table believes that the world business community should play an important role in improving economic and social conditions. As a statement of aspirations, this document aims to express a world standard against which business behavior can be measured. We seek to begin a process that identifies shared values, reconciles differing values, and thereby develops a shared perspective on business behavior acceptable to and honored by all.

These principles are rooted in two basic ethical ideals: kyosei and human dignity. The Japanese concept of kyosei means living and working together for the common good enabling cooperation and mutual prosperity to coexist with healthy and fair competition. "Human dignity" refers to the sacredness or value of each person as an end, not simply as a mean to the fulfillment of others' purposes or even majority prescription.

The General Principles in Section 2 seek to clarify the spirit of kyosei and "human dignity," while the specific Stakeholder Principles in Section 3 are concerned with their practical application.

In its language and form, the document owes a substantial debt to The Minnesota Principles, a statement of business behavior developed by the Minnesota Center for Corporate Responsibility. The Center hosted and chaired the drafting committee, which included Japanese, European, and United States representatives.

Business behavior can affect relationships among nations and the prosperity and well-being of us all. Business is often the first contact between nations and, by the way in which it causes social and economic changes, has a significant impact on the level of fear or confidence felt by people worldwide. Members of the Caux Round Table place their first emphasis on putting one's own house in order, and on seeking to establish what is right rather than who is right.

Section 1. Preamble

The mobility of employment, capital, products and technology is making business increasingly global in its transactions and its effects.

Law and market forces are necessary but insufficient guides for conduct.

Responsibility for the policies and actions of business and respect for the dignity and interests of its stakeholders are fundamental.

Shared values, including a commitment to shared prosperity, are as important for a global community as for communities of smaller scale.

For these reasons, and because business can be a powerful agent of positive social change, we offer the following principles as a foundation for dialogue and action by business leaders in search of business responsibility. In so doing, we affirm the necessity for moral values in business decision making. Without them, stable business relationships and a sustainable world community are impossible.

Section 2. General Principles

Principle 1. The Responsibilities Of Businesses: *Beyond Shareholders toward Stakeholders*
The value of a business to society is the wealth and employment it creates and the marketable products and services it provides to consumers at a reasonable price commensurate with quality. To create such value, a business must maintain its own economic health and viability, but survival is not a sufficient goal.

Businesses have a role to play in improving the lives of all their customers, employees, and shareholders by sharing with them the wealth they have created. Suppliers and competitors as well should expect businesses to honor their obligations in a spirit of honesty and fairness. As responsible citizens of the local, national, regional and global communities in which they operate, businesses share a part in shaping the future of those communities.

Principle 2. The Economic and Social Impact of Business: *Toward Innovation, Justice and World Community*
Businesses established in foreign countries to develop, produce or sell should also contribute to the social advancement of those countries by creating productive employment and helping to raise the purchasing power of their citizens. Businesses also should contribute to human rights, education, welfare, and vitalization of the countries in which they operate.

Businesses should contribute to economic and social development not only in the countries in which they operate, but also in the world community at large, through effective and prudent use of resources, free and fair competition, and emphasis upon innovation in technology, production methods, marketing and communications.

Principle 3. Business Behavior: *Beyond the Letter of Law Toward a Spirit of Trust*
While accepting the legitimacy of trade secrets, businesses should recognize that sincerity, candor, truthfulness, the keeping of promises, and transparency contribute not only to their own credibility and stability but also to the smoothness and efficiency of business transactions, particularly on the international level.

Principle 4. Respect for Rules
To avoid trade frictions and to promote freer trade, equal conditions for competition, and fair and equitable treatment for all participants, businesses should respect international and domestic rules. In addition, they should recognize that some behavior, although legal, may still have adverse consequences.

Principle 5. Support for Multilateral Trade
Businesses should support the multilateral trade systems of the GATT/World Trade Organization and similar international agreements. They should cooperate in efforts to promote the progressive and judicious liberalization of trade and to relax those domestic measures that unreasonably hinder global commerce, while giving due respect to national policy objectives.
Principle 6. Respect for the Environment
A business should protect and, where possible, improve the environment, promote sustainable development, and prevent the wasteful use of natural resources.

Principle 6. Respect for the Environment
A business should protect and, where possible, improve the environment, promote sustainable development, and prevent the wasteful use of natural resources.

130

Principle 7. Avoidance of Illicit Operations
A business should not participate in or condone bribery, money laundering, or other corrupt practices: indeed, it should seek cooperation with others to eliminate them. It should not trade in arms or other materials used for terrorist activities, drug traffic or other organized crime.

Section 3. Stakeholder Principles

Customers
We believe in treating all customers with dignity, irrespective of whether they purchase our products and services directly from us or otherwise acquire them in the market. We therefore have a responsibility to:

- provide our customers with the highest quality products and services consistent with their requirements;
- treat our customers fairly in all aspects of our business transactions, including a high level of service and remedies for their dissatisfaction;
- make every effort to ensure that the health and safety of our customers, as well as the quality of their environment, will be sustained or enhanced by our products and services;
- assure respect for human dignity in products offered, marketing, and advertising; and respect the integrity of the culture of our customers.

Employees
We believe in the dignity of every employee and in taking employee interests seriously. We therefore have a responsibility to:

- provide jobs and compensation that improve workers' living conditions;
- provide working conditions that respect each employee's health and dignity;
- be honest in communications with employees and open in sharing information, limited only by legal and competitive constraints;
- listen to and, where possible, act on employee suggestions, ideas, requests and complaints;
- engage in good faith negotiations when conflict arises;
- avoid discriminatory practices and guarantee equal treatment and opportunity in areas such as gender, age, race, and religion;
- promote in the business itself the employment of differently abled people in places of work where they can be genuinely useful;
- protect employees from avoidable injury and illness in the workplace;
- encourage and assist employees in developing relevant and transferable skills and knowledge; and
- be sensitive to the serious unemployment problems frequently associated with business decisions, and work with governments, employee groups, other agencies and each other in addressing these dislocations.

Owners / Investors
We believe in honoring the trust our investors place in us. We therefore have a responsibility to:

- apply professional and diligent management in order to secure a fair and competitive return on our owners' investment;
- disclose relevant information to owners/investors subject to legal requirements and competitive constraints;
- conserve, protect, and increase the owners/investors' assets; and

- respect owners/investors' requests, suggestions, complaints, and formal resolutions.

Suppliers
Our relationship with suppliers and subcontractors must be based on mutual respect. We therefore have a responsibility to:

- seek fairness and truthfulness in all our activities, including pricing, licensing, and rights to sell;
- ensure that our business activities are free from coercion and unnecessary litigation;
- foster long-term stability in the supplier relationship in return for value, quality, competitiveness and reliability;
- share information with suppliers and integrate them into our planning processes;
- pay suppliers on time and in accordance with agreed terms of trade; and
- seek, encourage and prefer suppliers and subcontractors whose employment practices respect human dignity.

Competitors
We believe that fair economic competition is one of the basic requirements for increasing the wealth of nations and ultimately for making possible the just distribution of goods and services. We therefore have a responsibility to:

- foster open markets for trade and investment;
- promote competitive behavior that is socially and environmentally beneficial and demonstrates mutual respect among competitors;
- refrain from either seeking or participating in questionable payments or favors to secure competitive advantages;
- respect both tangible and intellectual property rights; and
- refuse to acquire commercial information by dishonest or unethical means, such as industrial espionage.

Communities
We believe that as global corporate citizens we can contribute to such forces of reform and human rights as are at work in the communities in which we operate. We therefore have a responsibility in those communities to:

- respect human rights and democratic institutions, and promote them wherever practicable;
- recognize government's legitimate obligation to the society at large and support public policies and practices that promote human development through harmonious relations between business and other segments of society;
- collaborate with those forces in the community dedicated to raising standards of health, education, workplace safety and economic well-being;
- promote and stimulate sustainable development and play a leading role in preserving and enhancing the physical environment and conserving the earth's resources;
- support peace, security, diversity and social integration;
- respect the integrity of local cultures; and
- be a good corporate citizen through charitable donations, educational and cultural contributions, and employee participation in community and civic affairs.

Appendix III – How Not to Learn Lean Management [1]

It is common for companies to experience many difficulties implementing Lean management. After three to five years, the CEO or president will often seek to hire a senior manager to correct the problem. They will look for someone with Lean implementation experience to lead the company's Lean transformation. However, doing this will not correct the fundamental problem. Hiring a Lean implementation leader will be a mistake because you cannot learn Lean management by delegating it to someone else. And you will certainly add cost to the business by hiring another vice president.

The job descriptions of Lean implementation leaders, typically co-written by hiring companies and executive search firms, offer interesting insights into how they view Lean management and how to lead a Lean transformation. The following is an example of an actual job search announcement. While most people would find the job description very well done, closer inspection reveals many serious problems.

Your assignment is to determine what is wrong with this job description. Specifically, you should scrutinize the senior management team's views with regard to roles and responsibilities and what it takes to successfully lead a Lean transformation. The answers appear at the end of this section.

Job Description - Lean Implementation Leader
The role of the Vice President will be to bring an accelerated Lean program to the entire organization.

What are the problems here?

-

-

The Vice President will have responsibility for building the Lean organization, training the personnel and coordinating the activities of an enterprise-wide continuous improvement program.

What are the problems here?

-

-

Current understanding and practices of Lean must be augmented and implementation must be accelerated. To these ends senior management has elected to create this position that will have full focus on Lean deployment.

What are the problems here?

-

-

The Vice President will initially create a strategy and plan for implementation along with the senior officers of the company. As this plan will affect all functions of the organization it is imperative that the officer obtain buy in from those concerned.

What are the problems here?

-
-

It is anticipated that the plan be available for tactical deployment within the first 3 to 6 months.

What are the problems here?

-
-

Metrics development for process monitoring is the responsibility of the Vice president.

What are the problems here?

-
-

Candidate should be able to produce quantifiable results including reductions in inventories, working capital reduction, increased service levels and improved operating profit and cash flow.

What are the problems here?

-
-

Experience in culture change and Lean installation on a company-wide basis is required. We are aware of the need to conduct improvement and change throughout the organization. A sense of timing and an understanding of the ramifications of each change on the organization as a whole are needed in this individual.

What are the problems here?

-
-

We envision this individual as a team builder. Change of this magnitude will not be successful unless the Vice President is capable of building strong team commitment for change and improvement throughout the organization. Our candidate of choice will have a proven record of coalescing attitudes for change.

What are the problems here?

-

-

MBA Degree.

What are the problems here?

-

-

Answers to Appendix III Exercise

The role of the Vice President will be to bring an accelerated Lean program to the entire organization.

The problems are:
- Lean is a management system, not a program.
- A single vice president cannot accelerate Lean implementation. This places an unreasonable expectation on the VP, and will likely lead to poor outcomes or even failure. It takes the dedicated efforts of the entire senior management team, led by the CEO or president to achieve a Lean transformation.
- Using the term "accelerated" can imply that the company will soon be Lean, when in fact a company is never Lean, since there is no end to continuous improvement.

The Vice President will have responsibility for building the Lean organization, training the personnel and coordinating the activities of an enterprise-wide continuous improvement program.

The problems are:
- Responsibility for building a Lean organization lies with the entire senior management team, led by the CEO or President.
- Each senior manager has the responsibility for training personnel, which is gained through direct participation in kaizen.

Current understanding and practices of Lean must be augmented and implementation must be accelerated. To these ends senior management has elected to create this position that will have full focus on Lean deployment.

The problems are:
- Each senior manager should be fully focused on Lean implementation if they truly expect implementation efforts to be accelerated.

The Vice President will initially create a strategy and plan for implementation along with the senior officers of the company. As this plan will affect all functions of the organization it is imperative that the officer obtain buy in from those concerned.

The problems are:
- If senior management has elected to create this position, then it is odd that the vice president would have to be saddled with the requirement to obtain buy-in from those who presumably support the activities associated with this position.
- Having to gain buy-in among senior officers will slow down the Lean implementation, contradicting the need for accelerating implementation.

It is anticipated that the plan be available for tactical deployment within the first 3 to 6 months.

The problems are:
- Lean implementation must be connected to company strategy. The wording implies that Lean deployment can be independent of company strategy.
- Planning and justifications consume time, thus contradicting the stated need for accelerating implementation.

Metrics development for process monitoring is the responsibility of the Vice president.

The problems are:
- Developing new metrics for process monitoring can result in: a) the proliferation of metrics, many of which will conflict with established metrics, b) unnecessary complexity, or both.
- Ownership for business metrics is distributed among the senior management team. Current metrics should be examined for consistency with Lean principles and practices. Many will be eliminated and replaced with fewer, simpler metrics that give real-time visibility into the performance of workflows. This requires the involvement of all senior managers.
- Making the vice president solely responsible for metrics development and process monitoring places an unreasonable expectation on the vice president, and will likely lead to poor outcomes or even failure.

Candidate should be able to produce quantifiable results including reductions in inventories, working capital reduction, increased service levels and improved operating profit and cash flow.

The problems are:
- This wording implies that deployment of Lean principles and practices should be limited to operations, and the reason for implementing Lean is mostly financial.
- The reason for implementing Lean is to improve end-use customer satisfaction and becoming a better time-based competitor, which leads to improved financial results.
- Improved financial and non-financial results are achieved by improving workflows across functions and between companies (i.e. customers and suppliers). It is not the sole responsibility of one vice president.
- Improved financials and higher stock price are the byproduct of improving the non-financial performance of value-adding activities.

Experience in culture change and Lean installation on a company-wide basis is required. We are aware of the need to conduct improvement and change throughout the organization. A sense of timing and an understanding of the ramifications of each change on the organization as a whole are needed in this individual.

The problems are:
- The words "culture change" are often subject to interpretation in Lean transformations. It is most often associated with changes in how specific work activities are performed, with little or no emphasis on management's beliefs or behaviors. What is needed is a change in the dozens of beliefs among all senior managers, which then results in behaviors and competencies that support Lean principles and practices. This establishes the basis for wider organizational support of the Lean management system.
- Having "a sense of timing and an understanding of the ramifications of each change" contradicts the need for accelerating implementation.

We envision this individual as a team builder. Change of this magnitude will not be successful unless the Vice President is capable of building strong team commitment for change and improvement throughout the organization. Our candidate of choice will have a proven record of coalescing attitudes for change.

The problems are:
- Conventional business metrics focus on point optimization and discourage cross-functional teamwork. So does an environment based on fear and blame, as well as layoffs due to productivity improvement. The vice president will be unable to successfully promote team building in the absence of a no-blame policy, qualified job guarantee, and metrics that are fully aligned with Lean principles and practices. This will contradict the need for accelerating implementation.
- Is it reasonable to expect the vice president to be able to coalesce attitudes for change when the current senior managers have apparently been unsuccessful at achieving this requirement?

MBA Degree.

The problems are:
- Business schools do not teach the Lean management system throughout their MBA curriculum. In fact, most of what they teach is the opposite of Lean.
- MBA degrees are of little value with respect to leading a Lean transformation. What counts is deep on-the-job experience in practicing "Continuous Improvement" and "Respect for People" at the point where value-added work is actually performed.

Appendix III – Self-Study
Write your responses in the space provided.

 Thinking and **Doing**

1. Write a job description for an executive that does not suffer any of the shortcomings described in the previous section and is fully consistent with Lean principles.

About the Author

M.L. "Bob" Emiliani is currently a professor at Connecticut State University in New Britain, Conn., where he teaches various courses on Lean management.

Prior to that Bob worked in the consumer products and aerospace industries for nearly two decades. He held management positions in engineering, manufacturing, and supply chain management, and had responsibility for implementing Lean in manufacturing operations and supply chains.

He has authored or co-authored a dozen papers related to Lean leadership including: "Lean Behaviors" (1998), "Linking Leaders' Beliefs to their Behaviors and Competencies" (2003), "Using Value Stream Maps to Improve Leadership" (2004), "Origins of Lean Management in America: The Role of Connecticut Businesses" (2006), and "Standardized Work for Executive Leadership (2008). Five of his papers have won awards for excellence.

Bob is the principal author of the book *Better Thinking, Better Results: Case Study and Analysis of an Enterprise-Wide Lean Transformation*, (second edition, 2007), a detailed case study and analysis of The Wiremold Company's Lean transformation from 1991 to 2001. It won a Shingo Research Prize in 2003 as the first book to describe an enterprise-wide Lean transformation in a real company where both principles of Lean management – "Continuous Improvement" and "Respect for People" – were applied.

He is also the author of *REAL LEAN: Understanding the Lean Management System* (Volume One) and *REAL LEAN: Critical Issues and Opportunities in Lean Management* (Volume Two), both published in 2007; and *REAL LEAN: The Keys to Sustaining Lean Management* (Volume Three), published in 2008.

Bob earned engineering degrees from the University of Miami, University of Rhode Island, and Brown University.

He is a principal of The Center for Lean Business Management, LLC. (www.theclbm.com).

PRACTICAL LEAN LEADERSHIP

"...employees are offering a very important part of their life to us. If we don't use their time effectively, we are wasting their lives." – Eiji Toyoda

Lean Management System

A non-zero-sum principle-based management system focused on creating value for end-use customers and eliminating waste, unevenness, and unreasonableness using the scientific method.

Principles	Key Objectives	Processes and Tools
• Continuous Improvement	• Respect for People	
• Create Value for Customers	• Balance / Harmony	
• Stable Long-Term Growth	• Innovation	

Processes and Tools

- 5S
- A3 Reports
- Just-In-Time
- Kaizen
- Percent Loading Charts
- Policy Deployment
- Product-Quantity Analysis
- Quality Function Deployment
- Root Cause Analysis
- Standardized Work
- Statistical Process Control
- Takt Time
- Total Productive Maintenance
- Value Stream Maps
- Visual Workplace
- Work Cells

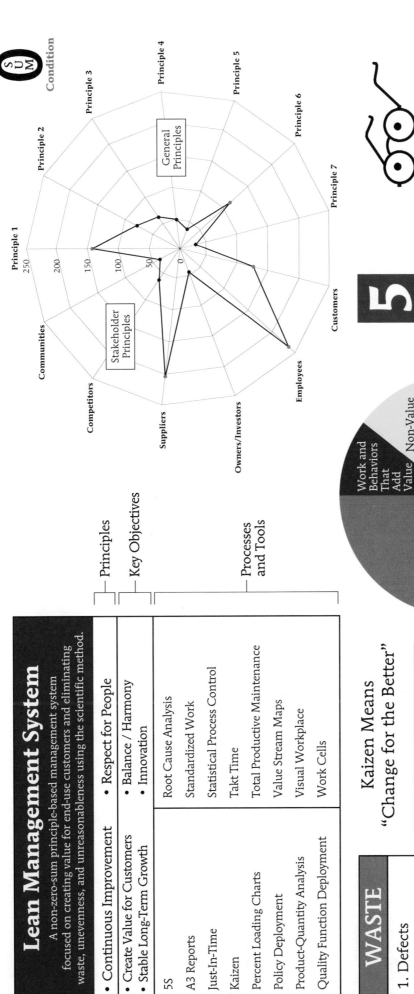

Abnormal Condition S/U/M

General Principles — Principle 1, Principle 2, Principle 3, Principle 4, Principle 5, Principle 6, Principle 7

Stakeholder Principles — Communities, Competitors, Suppliers, Owners/Investors, Employees, Customers

It's OK to Share

5 Whys

Kaizen Means "Change for the Better"

Kaizen Principles:
- Process and Results
- Systems Focus
- Non-Blaming, Non-Judgemental

Pie chart:
- Work and Behaviors That Add Value
- Non-Value Added But Necessary Work and Behaviors
- Waste

WASTE

1. Defects
2. Transportation
3. Overproduction
4. Waiting
5. Processing
6. Movement
7. Inventory
8. Behaviors

PRACTICAL LEAN LEADERSHIP

"...employees are offering a very important part of their life to us. If we don't use their time effectively, we are wasting their lives." – Eiji Toyoda

Value-Added Behaviors

Value-Added Behaviors	Behavioral Waste®
Humility	Blame
Calmness	Office Politics
Wisdom	Confusion
Patience	Inconsistency
Objectivity	Unknown Expectations
Balance	Revenge
Trust	Elitism

Lean Behaviors®

1. Specify Value
I seek to understand the expectations of people I interact with regardless of position or status. I consider the perspectives of key stakeholders (associates, suppliers, customers, investors, community).

2. Identify the Value Stream
I understand which of my behaviors add value and which are waste, and how my behaviors impact business processes and value creation for end-use customers. I strive to achieve non-zero-sum gains.

3. Flow
I understand how my leadership behaviors can create errors, delays, confusion, and re-work. I think about how to do my work in less time to help improve work flows. I am not an impediment to information flow.

4. Pull
I understand the pull signals that my key stakeholders give me. I strive to do what is wanted, when it is wanted, in the amount wanted, and where it is wanted.

5. Continuous Improvement
I work to eliminate behavioral waste. I continuously improve my understanding of behavioral waste and strive to eliminate it to facilitate information flow.

Leadership Belief
Something accepted as true.

→ **Leadership Behavior**
Conduct based on beliefs.

→ **Leadership Competency**
An established skill or capability.

Continuous Personal Improvement

One-Piece Flow
I understand the value-added part of my work. I am able to perform my work as it comes to me, mostly without delay. I think of how to eliminate waste in my own daily activities.

Standardized Work
I am consistent in my words and actions. I strive to reduce variation in interpretation of my intent. I treat people the same regardless of level.

Kanban
I respond to signals from stakeholders to provide what is needed, when it is needed, in the amount needed, and where it is needed.

The Five S's
My mind, work habits, and workplace are well-organized.

Visual Controls
I seek to eliminate facial expressions and body language that signal disinterest or distrust.

Audio Signals
The tone, volume, pace, inflection, and timing of my voice is used effectively to signal positive interest or support.

Total Productive Maintenance
I try to improve my personal effectiveness by maintaining my mind and body. I achieve good balance between work, family, and personal interests.

Standardized Work for Executive Leadership

1. Leadership Definition	Beliefs, behaviors, and competencies that demonstrate respect for people, motivate people, improve business conditions, minimize or eliminate organizational politics, ensure effective utilization of resources, and eliminate confusion and rework.
2. Business Principles	Caux Round Table *Principles for Business* • Seven General Principles • Six Stakeholder Principles
3. Standard Skill Set	Customer First; Process and Results; Developing People; Quantitative plus Qualitative; Go See / Get Hands Dirty; PDCA Cycle; Root Cause Analysis; Time Consciousness; Stakeholders as Resources, Not Costs; Technology to Help People; Sharing

Fifty Errors

54351400R00085

Made in the USA
Charleston, SC
30 March 2016